Desires

Characteristics of True Conversion

David Wayne Meeker

Desires

Characteristics of True Conversion

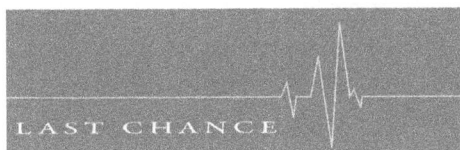

Published by Last Chance Music Ministry

David Wayne Meeker

ELEVATION PRESS
OF COLORADO

DESIRES: Characteristics of True Conversion
by David Wayne Meeker

Editing services provided by Laura Diane Meeker
Cover and interior design and interior formatting by Donna Marie Benjamin of Elevation Press of Colorado.

Credits:
Dove icon used in title: Calvary Chapel Ministries; used by permission
Icons used in cover design: Freepik.com
Icons used in interior pages:
Preacher icon: Andrew Doane/thenounproject.com
Magnifying glass icon: alkhalifi design/freepik.com
Test icon: freepik.com
Black test icon: kerismaker/freepik.com
Steps icon: graphicmall / freepik.com
Lightbulb — Icon by HAJICON / freepik.com
Definitions – Icon by Good Ware / freepik.com
Back cover photo: Laura Diane Meeker

All Scriptures are *The Holy Bible, Berean Study Bible (BSB)*.
©2016, 2018 by Bible Hub, unless otherwise noted. Used by permission.

David & Laura Meeker
lastchancemusic1@aol.com

Ordering information: Quantity sales. Special discounts are available on quantity purchases by book clubs, corporations, associations, and others. For details, contact the publisher at the address above.

ISBN 979-8-9853834-4-7

1. Main category— [Bible] 2. Other categories— [Christian Living]— [True Conversion]

© 2024
Last Chance Music Ministry
lastchancemusic1@aol.com

Elevation Press of Colorado
Cedaredge, Colorado
www.elevation-press-books.com

Acknowledgements

I acknowledge the conumdrum of God
becoming flesh and celebrate in our
amazing salvation through Jesus Christ our Lord
Who will never leave us nor forsake us —
not even in Heaven before His Father!

·᚛ᚑᚌᚑ᚜·

Desires: Characteristics of True Conversion
is lovingly dedicated to all of the elect
who are currently in transition.

·᚛ᚑᚌᚑ᚜·

Desire

[dih-zahyuhr]

–verb

1. to wish or long for; crave; want

    –Dictionary.com

Consciousness

[kon-shuhs-nis]

–noun

1. Awareness of something for what it is; internal knowledge

    –Dictionary.com

Contents

A Word from
Last Chance Music Ministry

LCMM desires that all disciples of Christ will rightly divide the Word of Truth (2 Ti. 2:15); worship God in Spirit and in Truth (Jn. 4:24); be ready to give an answer to anyone who asks about the hope that is in us with gentleness and respect (1 Pe. 3:15); and love God with all our heart, mind, soul, and strength (Mk. 12:30).

This is why LCMM produces Christian books and Christian music to help believers draw closer to God through Jesus Christ, via the Holy Spirit. That is why the products we provide to our communities must meet certain criteria before ever reaching any person or group. The materials that we produce and distribute must glorify God, edify the Body of Christ, and reach a lost and dying world. Part of our ministry involves giving away various types and styles of Bibles — free of charge, in both English and many other languages. When you support LCMM by purchasing our books and music CDs, you enable us to produce more Christian materials and distribute them into the communities that need them. Thank you for supporting LCMM, and may God bless you!

Sincerely in Christ,
David & Laura Meeker

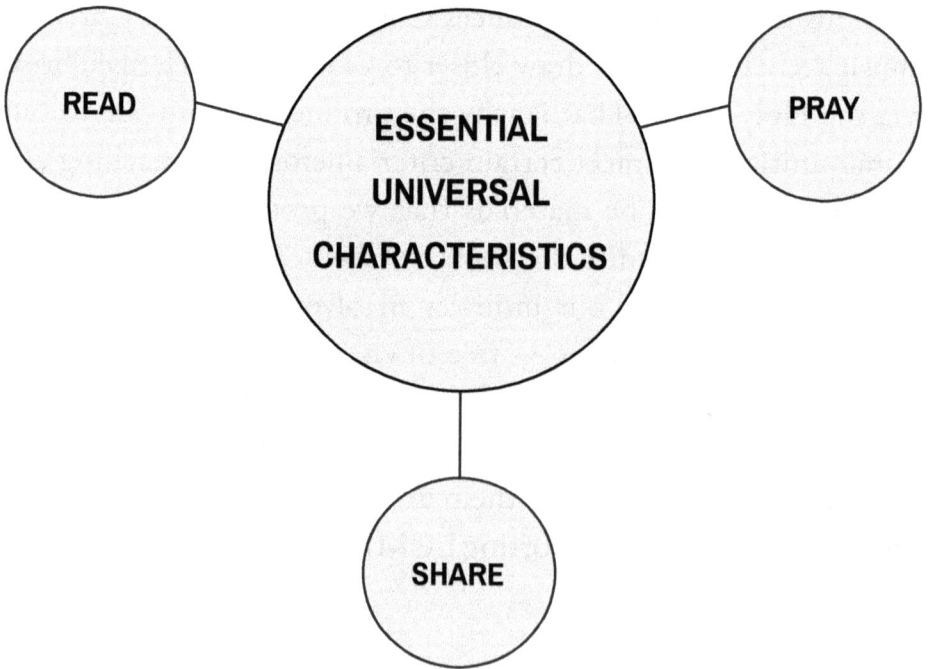

What are the Essential Universal Characteristics (EUCs)?

The Essential Universal Characteristics (EUCs) are three desires, that spiritually precede the physical manifestation of our God-glorifying good works, deeds, and actions which have been supernaturally implanted deep within our conscience (i.e. heart, mind, soul, and spirit) by God the Holy Spirit at the moment of our regeneration and justification experience (Tit. 3:1-8) — which are the byproducts and indicators of true saving faith (Ja. 2:14-26). Let me explain the meaning of each letter and their corresponding word usage in the acronym "EUC." The letter meanings and their corresponding definitions are as follows:

1. **E = ESSENTIAL.** The absolutely vital and necessary; in the highest sense with regard to importance.

2. **U = UNIVERSAL.** The commonality and applicability to all authentically regenerated Christian believers in the world as a whole and everywhere regardless of race, gender, and disabilities.

3. **C = CHARACTERISTICS.** Distinguishing features or qualities, traits, or attributes.

The EUCs acronym will help us to identify the byproducts and indicators of true saving faith as described within Scripture and outlined in the Essential Universal Characteristics EUCs. These three essential *desires* of the Christian faith that have been created, powered, and maintained by the work of God the Holy Spirit — that absolutely identify an authentic regeneration (i.e. true conversion) which can be found in all authentic conversions universally and globally, regardless of gender, race, or disabilities — are as follows:

1. Reading the Word of God daily (Ps. 1:1-2; 2 Ti. 2:15, 3:16-17).
2. Praying to God daily (Ep. 6:18; 1 Th. 5:16-18).
3. Sharing the Gospel of Jesus Christ regularly (Mt. 28:18-20; 1 Pe. 3:15).

The Absence

The main premise of *Desires: Characteristics of True Conversion* is that the absence of the three Essential Universal Characteristics (EUCs) in the life of a self-professing follower of Christ is irrefutable evidence of the *absence*, and lack of the presence of, God the Holy Spirit (Ja. 2:14). Christ told His disciples that you could identify His followers by their fruit, and that a good tree cannot bear bad fruit, and a bad tree cannot bear good fruit (Mt. 7:15-20; Ga. 5:22-23). Also, we must keep in mind that the fruit of God the Holy Spirit is also an effect and indicator of authentic regeneration and justification (i.e. true conversion). The fruits of true conversion involve beliefs, actions, and knowledge that will always be harmonious with the contents of the Word of God (Ro. 10:17). That is because true conversion is a work of God's sovereign grace in the heart of the adopted child of God (Jn. 1:12; Ro. 1:16). In the Heidelberg Catechism[1], the Reformed Churches equated "true repentance" with "conversion." The term *true conversion* describes the process of bringing individuals into a correct and proper relationship with God that involves the following necessary effects of authentic regeneration:

- Having extreme disgust and hatred for sin.
- Giving up and putting aside voluntarily the pleasures of the world.

---

1   https://www.crcna.org. Heidelberg Catechism (1563).

- Demolishing and destroying pride.
- Surrendering yourself to the will of God.
- Exercising your faith consistently with the teachings of Scripture.
- Recognizing Christ as the precious King and Savior.
- Receiving gladly and accepting willingly that the cross of Christ is one's only saving hope.

The Gifts

The Bible tells us that even repentance itself is a gift that God grants by His sovereign grace (Mt. 4:17; Ac. 3:19, 5:31, 11:18; Ro. 2:4; 2 Ti. 2:24-26). The Bible tells us that God turns the human heart to Himself (Jn. 6:44; Ro. 8:30; Ph. 1:6). The Bible also tells us that the Spirit of God is the sovereign cause of the new birth (Jn. 3:3; Ja. 1:18; 1 Pe. 1:3-4). God is so amazing! He also gives us the Gift of the Holy Spirit (Ac. 2:38-39). God also gives us righteousness as a gift (Ro. 5:17). He gives us the Gift of Eternal Life (Ro. 6:23). This is amazing because the Bible also tells us that in our natural carnal and fallen state we are deserving of hell (Ro. 3:23); but to the authentically regenerated people, God gives the Gift of Eternal Life (Ep. 2:8-9).

Again, the identification and application of the desires of the Essential Universal Characteristics (EUCs) in the Christian life are undeniably, and without question, evidence of authentic regeneration and justification (i.e. true conversion).

Embedded Desires

Prior to the regeneration and transformation of the human heart, the Bible tells us that the unregenerate heart is deceitfully wicked above all things (Jer. 17:9-10) and that many evil things come from within it (Mk. 7:21-23). That is why when we experience an authentic regeneration, God the Holy Spirit gives us a new heart (Ez. 36:26-27; Ps. 51:10; Ro. 12:2) — with new desires — desires that glorify God in doing His will, which include the things that we say, do, and think (Ps. 37:4-5; 2 Co. 5:9-11). Here are eight examples of how a newly transformed heart can please God in doing His will through the indwelling work and power of God the Holy Spirit in the life of an authentically regenerated believer:

1. Bearing fruit in good works, deeds, and actions (Col. 1:10).
2. Presenting your body as a living sacrifice to God (Ro. 12:1).
3. Looking out for your weaker brother (Ro. 15:1-2).
4. Truthfully teaching the Word of God (1 Th. 2:4).
5. Praying for those who are in authority (1 Ti. 2:1-3).
6. Supporting family members who are in need (1 Ti. 5:8).
7. Sharing with others who are in need (He. 13:16).
8. Keeping God's commandments (1 Jn. 3:22).

Transformed Heart

In order for the adopted children of God to accomplish the will of God and to please Him in our lives, we need a newly regenerated and transformed heart. The newly transformed heart causes a change in a person's nature or core identity, and the person becomes a new creation (2 Co. 5:17). Some of the effects that occur after authentic regeneration are outlined below:

1. Being declared righteous before God.
2. Having a desire to please God.

3. Being transformed into the image of God's Son, Jesus Christ, through the sanctification process.

4. Having your priorities, passions, and purpose all aligned with God's plan for your life.

5. Wanting what God wants and working towards it, even at a personal cost.

The Change

The Bible says that when God calls (1 Co. 1:9; 2 Co. 5:17; 2 Th. 2:14) those He chooses to regenerate (Mk. 13:20; Jn. 6:44; Ro. 8:28-30; Ep. 1:4-50) through His grace (Ep. 2:8-9), He gives the ability for the child of God to love Him above all else (Mt. 22:37) and to make God's desires harmonious with their heart's desires (Ps. 37:4). In other words, God's love for his elect precedes and enables their love toward Him. The elect are given the supernatural ability to respond to God's love and to choose Him. (Ps. 139:5-7; Ep. 1:4-14). The regenerated and transformed heart is responsible and necessary for the changes in our thoughts, attitudes, and actions (Pr. 21:1-3). Also, God gives His newly adopted children both the "things hoped for" and "things not yet seen" (He. 11:1).

A Personal Confirmation

When God the Holy Spirit communicates with the spirit of the regenerated child of God's conscience, it is a personal confirmation of now being a child of God (Ro. 8:14-17). The God-glorifying changes created within the heart of an authentically regenerated child of God will cause and facilitate repentance and obedience; and because of this, the newly regenerated child of God will immediately pursue the desires that the Holy Spirit implanted and will begin to apply them to everyday life (He. 6: 11-12). This can only be achieved by the adopted child of God through the work and power of God the Holy Spirit. Without the supernatural transforming effect of an authentic regeneration by God the Holy Spirit in our lives, our carnal and unregenerated heart cannot understand the things of the Spirit of God (Ro. 1:21, 8:7; 1 Co. 2:14; Ep. 4:18-19; He. 9:14). The phrase *being a child of God* is synonymous with being transformed, which is an effect of authentic regeneration. The evidence of the Holy Spirit's imbedded spiritual desires working alongside with the physically manifested evidence of our God-glorifying good works, deeds, and actions as outlined in Scripture and the EUCs are the byproducts and indicators of true saving faith within the life of a believer: there is no plausible explanation that could be presented to explain their absence — apart from the absence of God the Holy Spirit. Without the manifestation of the EUCs, there is no real spiritual and physical evidence by which we could identify, to ourselves or to others, the proof of God the Holy Spirit's work of regeneration and justification and its effect — true conversion — none!

Reasonable Explanation

As I briefly mentioned previously, another truth of the EUCs is that genuine regeneration (i.e. spiritual resurrection) by God the Holy Spirit produces — supernaturally within us — a new heart, mind, soul, and spirit, also known as a new conscience (Tit. 3:4-8; He. 10:22; 1 Jn. 1:9); and because of this, a believer will absolutely exhibit God-glorifying *desires* that are consistent with, and necessary for, the personal application of our God-glorifying good works, deeds, and actions — specifically the personal application of the three *desires* of the EUCs as outlined in this book (i.e. read, pray, and share). If we believe that God is truly God (Is. 45:5) and that He has saved us through grace by faith in Jesus Christ (Ro. 3:21-28; Ep. 2:8), then why would we not exhibit the *desires* to please and obey Him? There can only be one reasonable explanation for this. This reason can only be logically attributive to the absence of the work of God the Holy Spirit in the regeneration process (i.e. false conversion). I believe that this truth is the underlying foundation of James Chapter 2 — specifically verses 14 and 26 — which, based on my observation, is one of the most misunderstood books, chapters, and verses in the entire Bible.

Can and Cannot Do

At this point, I would like to clarify to you, the reader, what the EUCs *"can do"* — and what the EUCs *"cannot do."* The EUCs cannot achieve nor are they a means to salvation itself, but rather are the evidence of our God-glorifying good works, deeds, and actions, including the application of the EUCs in our daily life, which are the byproducts and indicators of true saving faith. God-glorifying good works, deeds, and actions are a clear and obvious indicator in identifying and determining authentic regeneration and its effect — true conversion. Again, the EUCs cannot, and will not, ever earn us salvation in and of themselves. In other words, works are not the means to salvation — they are the result of salvation. Let me explain it to you another way. Good works, deeds, and actions are a manifestation of our transformation. Our God-glorifying good works, deeds, and actions are not the cause or the reason for our transformation. Regeneration is the cause and the reason for our transformation. Good works, deeds, and actions are the byproducts, indicators, and effects of our transformation.

Personal Identification

Desires: Characteristics of True Conversion is about how to personally identify the deep spiritual *desires* that precede the physical manifestation of our God-glorifying good works, deeds, and actions, and most importantly includes the application of the three EUCs as identified in Scripture and outlined in this book. The renewed and transformed heart (Ro. 12:1-2; 2 Co. 3:18) has been implanted deep within our conscience by God the Holy Spirit at the moment of our regeneration and justification (Tit. 3:1-8), which provides us with the irrefutable and undeniable evidences necessary to personally determine and identify that we really have had an authentic regeneration, justification, and sanctification (i.e. true conversion).

Time and Eternity

God-glorifying good works, deeds, and actions will play a very important and significant role in our Christian experience for both time and eternity in that they are not only the byproducts, indicators, and evidence of true saving faith but also of the faithfully, committed, and obedient children of God (Ro. 8:16-17). True children of God will actually get rewarded as a result of our good works, deeds, and actions when we arrive at the Judgment Seat of Christ in Heaven(Mt. 5:11-12; 1 Co. 3:8).

Wow! As if receiving the gift of salvation, eternal life, a new glorified body, spirit, and soul (1 Co. 15:51-55; 1 Th. 5:23-24); and fellowship with the Triune God throughout eternity (Jn. 3:16-18; Re. 21:1-4), in a place that Christ has prepared for us (Jn. 14:2-6), isn't enough. On top of that, the Triune God rewards us for the good behavior we exhibit that can only be accomplished by and through His work in us, which is the only way we can achieve any God-glorifying good works, deeds, and actions!

According to our Works

The Scriptures are very clear that both believers and non-believers will be judged according to their works (Ps. 62:12; Pr. 24:12; Jer. 17:10, 32:19; Mt. 16:27; Jn. 5:28-29; Ro. 2:6, 14:12; Re. 2:23, 22:12). Again, when regeneration occurs, God the Holy Spirit implants within the newly adopted child of God a new conscience (i.e. a new heart, soul, and spirit), which includes a new will, affections, and desires, that enables the newly adopted child of God to please and glorify God in the things we say, do, and think (Ps. 51:10; Is. 40:31; Ez. 36:26; Ro. 12:1-2; 2 Co. 5:17; Ep. 4:22-24; Ph. 1:6).

The Bema Seat

The Judgment Seat of Christ (i.e. Bema Seat), is described in Scripture in 2 Corinthians 5:10. It is the place where all Christians will be judged and rewarded for their God-glorifying good works, deeds, and actions. This judgment will not have anything to do with acquiring salvation itself, but rather it will have to do with the giving and taking away of rewards. It is exclusively for the believers who have been authentically regenerated and justified (i.e. truly converted).

No Indicators

If a self-professing follower of Christ does not exhibit both the supernaturally caused spiritual *desires* and the physical manifestation of God-glorifying good works, deeds, and actions, which include the personal application of the three essential EUCs in a believer's life, as I mentioned before, then there would be absolutely no indicators, or evidence, that could be presented to substantiate the claims of the self-professing believer as being authentically converted (i.e. regenerated and justified). We need to pay attention to the specific and essential byproducts and indicators of true saving faith as outlined in Scripture and within the parameters of the EUCs. This means that if the spiritual and physical manifestation of God-pleasing desires in the life of a self-professing believer does not, in fact, exist then there is absolutely no evidence being presented as proof of an authentic regeneration (i.e. true conversion) — none!

Without Evidence

Put simply, if a self-professing Christian cannot produce *"any"* of the evidences of the three essential *desires* found within Scripture and outlined in the EUCs, then he or she has not been regenerated by the Holy Spirit (meaning the person has a false conversion), which can only be positively identified through the spiritual along with the physical manifestation of our good works, deeds, and actions, as stipulated in God's Word and outlined in the EUCs.

The Whole Reason

This is the whole reason why I wrote *Desires: Characteristics of True Conversion* — to bring attention to the Christian Church this important truth about personally examining ourselves to see if, in fact, we are truly in the faith, just as the Apostle Paul commanded in 2 Corinthians 13:5:

"⁵Examine yourselves to see whether you are in the faith; test yourselves. Can't you see for yourselves that Jesus Christ is in you—unless you actually fail the test?"

I hope and pray that this above explanation helped you to better understand what the Essential Universal Characteristics EUCs are (and what they are not) and my reason for writing this book! God Bless you!

TO THE READER

Desires: Characteristics of True Conversion is a small book which invites the reader to explore and identify the *cause, method, and effects* of true conversion at a personal level. As previously mentioned, this book is not about achieving salvation through our good works, deeds, and actions in of themselves, but rather it is a book about both the spiritual and physical manifestations that are necessary and working together in achieving and identifying authentic conversion (i.e. regeneration). We want to focus on the spiritual *desires* that are manifested prior to the actual physical manifestations of our good works, deeds, and actions that have been supernaturally embedded within us by God the Holy Spirit at the moment of our regeneration and justification (Ro. 5:5; Ep. 3:17; Ga. 4:6; Tit. 3:1-8). The logical sequence of the salvation process explained in this book is that spiritual *desires* will always precede the physical manifestation of those preceding spiritual *desires*. It is the spiritual desires that are found deep within our conscience that precede the evidence of the physical manifestation of our good works, deeds, and actions which are the necessary indicators for determining the authenticity of our regeneration and justification (i.e. true conversion).

I feel it is important for me to specifically bring to your attention the spiritual reality of the supernatural *desires* that precede our good works, deeds, and actions. These desires are identified in this book as the three *Essential Universal Characteristics (EUCs)* that were implanted by God the Holy Spirit deep within our conscience at the moment of our regeneration and justification (Tit. 3:1-8). I believe that the spiritual and physical manifestation of our God-glorifying good works, deeds, and actions are synonymous with the work and presence of God the Holy Spirit and their absence is not!

Logical Sequence

Because of the importance of identifying and understanding the significance of the spiritual desires that precede the physical manifestations (i.e. God-glorifying good works, deeds, and actions), let me explain in five statements to help you better understand the logical sequence and significance of both the spiritual and physical desires and how they are intertwined together in the identification of authentic regeneration. Their logical sequence and significance are as follows:

1. If the existence and application of the spiritually embedded desires are never identified and implemented, then the physical manifestation of those preceding desires do not exist either.

2. If the physical manifestations of the initial spiritual desires do not exist, then the positive and accurate identification of an authentic regeneration does not exist.

3. If the positive and accurate identification of an authentic regeneration does not exist, then the positive evidence of the work of God the Holy Spirit also does not exist.

4. If the positive evidence of the work of God the Holy Spirit does not exist, then the byproducts and indicators of true conversion also do not exist.

5. If the byproducts and indicators of true conversion do not exist, then the reality of a non-saving faith is positively identified.

We can only positively identify authentic regeneration (i.e. true conversion) through the Holy Spirit-caused spiritual and physical manifestations of our God-glorifying good works, deeds, and actions which include the application of the three *Essential Universal Characteristics (EUCs)*.

The Counterfeit

Also, I want to point out to you, the reader, that due to the possibility that a counterfeit manifestation of an apparent conversion can occur for whatever reason or motive, the accurate identification of a true conversion can only be effectively identified at a personal level through the heart and conscience of the individual who has confessed to an authentic conversion (Ga. 1:6-9; Jude 1:4). That is the reason why the readers of this book, *Desires: Characteristics of True Conversion,* must absolutely be honest with themselves and to God in order to positively and correctly identify if, in fact, they are truly converted (i.e. authentically regenerated) and trusting in Christ alone for their salvation (Jn. 14:6; Ac. 4:12; Ro. 6:23; Ep. 2:8-9).

Words and Phrases

Let us look at the Biblical usage of the word *regeneration.* One of the many ways regeneration is referred to in the Bible is as a "second birth." Let me explain further. When Christians authentically believe and trust in Jesus Christ for their salvation, the Scriptures tell us they become born of God (1 Jn. 5:1) or born again (Jn. 3:3). The Apostle Paul tells us that we become a new creation (2 Co. 5:17). These words or phrases all describe the effects of the same cause — regeneration! In His conversation with Nicodemus, Christ refers to being "born again" as the only way to enter into the kingdom of God (Jn. 3:3-5). Jesus said that no one can see the kingdom of God unless they are born of water and the Spirit. Flesh is born of flesh, but spirit is born of Spirit. Let me explain this truth in another way:

1. "Born of water" refers to "physical birth."
2. "Born of the Spirit" refers to "Spiritual rebirth."
3. "Spiritual rebirth refers to "regeneration."
4. "Regeneration" refers to "true conversion."

The Spiritual rebirth that Christ was talking about is the effect of regeneration, which means that regeneration is necessary for our salvation (i.e. true conversion). Another result of regeneration is peace with God (Ro. 5:1). Regeneration will immediately produce justification; and also, at the same moment, the sanctification process will begin (Ro. 8:28-30). One of the difficulties in identifying true conversion is that the proof of true conversion can only be correctly and accurately identified within the circumference of the three *Essential Universal Characteristics (EUCs)* as they are revealed to us in Scripture and outlined through this book, *Desires: Characteristics of True Conversion.*

Foundational and Fundamental

True conversion cannot be determined by any other means apart from both the spiritual and the physical manifestations working together in achieving our God-glorifying good works, deeds, and actions, which include the personal application of the EUCs in the Christian life. That is because the EUCs are foundationally and fundamentally important teachings which are revealed to us in Scripture that instruct us about commitment, sacrifice, and obedience within our relationship with the Triune God, and include these three essential commands: **1.)** Read the

Word of God, **2.)** Communicate with God through prayer, and **3.)** Share the Gospel of Jesus Christ to a lost and dying world.

The Commands

The foregoing are three essential commands determined and assigned by God as requirements (i.e. works and actions) in the relationship between us and Him, which pleases and glorifies Him, as we are committed and obedient in doing His will. We come to Him through His Son, Jesus Christ, Who is the Only Mediator between God and men (1 Ti. 2:5) and the only name under heaven given by which men can be saved (Ac. 4:12), through the *desires* that have been implanted deep within our conscience by God the Holy Spirit (Tit. 3:1-8), at the moment of our regeneration and justification (Ga. 2:16, 3:24), Who is the Supernatural cause of the *desires* that precede our obedience to Christ and the manifestation of our good works, deeds, and actions (Ez. 36:25-27; Jn. 3:3-8; Ac. 9:1-9, 22:6-11, 26:12-18), which are evidence of authentic regeneration and justification (i.e. true conversion). Therefore, we can know we are born again (i.e. truly converted).

Cause, Method, and Effects

The Holy Bible clearly identifies the *cause, method,* and *effects* of true conversion as a spiritual turning away from our sin and rebellion through repentance (Ac. 3:19; 2 Ti. 2:22) while simultaneously turning toward Jesus Christ for salvation (Jn. 14:6; Ep. 2:1-9), which are the works of God the Holy Spirit and the effects of regeneration within our union with Jesus Christ (Ro. 6:4-6; Ep. 2:5-6). We will explore and identify the *cause, method,* and *effects* of true conversion so that you can personally validate your conversion as being authentic.

Will Not and Cannot

In this book, we will identify three necessary elements of true conversion, which are referred to in this book as the *Essential Universal Characteristics (EUCs)*. A truly converted believer will supernaturally exhibit these three essential EUCs, but a false conversion will not. The reason a false conversion *will not* is because they *cannot*, without the Supernatural transforming effects of regeneration and its imbedded desires (1 Co. 2:14).

I want you to honestly ask yourself these three questions regarding the EUCs: **1.)** Do I have a *desire* to read the Holy Bible daily? **2.)** Do I have a *desire* to pray to God daily? and **3.)** Do I have a *desire* to share the Gospel of Jesus Christ regularly?

The honest answers to these three EUC questions will give you a truthful understanding to the authenticity of your conversion.

The Struggle

Please keep in mind while you are reading *Desires: Characteristics of True Conversion* that we are all imperfect human beings dealing with our sinful nature on a daily basis. Our flesh will struggle against our newly regenerated spirit until we receive our resurrected and glorified bodies at the *End of the Age*. Until then, as a consequence of Adam and Eve's rebellion, all humanity now has a sinful nature, and we must factor into the equation the effects of our sinful nature with the EUCs: the *desires* of the flesh are against the Spirit, and the *desires* of the Spirit are against the flesh (Mt. 7:13-14; Ro. 7:18-25, 8:5-28; Ga. 5:17; 1 Jn. 2:16).

Let me explain to you, the reader, the relevance of the term *The Sinful Nature Factor* in a slightly different way. Because of the sinful nature and its temporary effect on our flesh (Ro. 7:13-25) — that is until we receive our glorified resurrected bodies at the

End of the Age (1 Co. 15:42-49; Ph. 3:21; 1 Jn. 3:2), the spiritual desires that precede the physical manifestations are a much more accurate and reliable method of identification in determining — at a personal level — the authenticity of our regeneration. This is because the spiritual desires that God the Holy Spirit has implanted deep within the conscience at the moment of our regeneration and justification are Holy Spirit-caused, powered, and maintained *desires,* which are a much more accurate and reliable source for identifying the authenticity of our God-glorifying good works, deeds, and actions as outlined in Scripture and the EUCs. Because of this work of the Holy Spirit, our spiritual desires have a much greater level of accuracy in determining authenticity, than the physical manifestation of our flesh, concerning our desires by themselves.

Also, the physical manifestations of our *desires* are simply the result and effect of the consistent and reliable Holy Spirit-caused and powered preceding spiritual desires. That is why we must identify the preceding spiritual desires in our Christian life at a personal level — first and foremost. Let me explain to you what I mean in this way:

- Spiritual Desires — Holy Spirit-caused, powered, and embedded spiritual desires are a more accurate and reliable method of identification that is found deep within the conscience, which is a better and more precise method of identification at a personal level for the positive identification and authenticity of true regeneration found deep within our conscience.
- Physical Desires — These are an effect of the Holy Spirit-caused and powered spiritual desires that are found deep within the conscience, which can be physically affected by

our sinful nature, and at times can be inaccurate, inconsistent, and unreliable as a sole source for the identification of authentic regeneration. The physical manifestations alone (by themselves) can also be easily counterfeited and manipulated knowingly or unknowingly for whatever reason or motive. In other words, without the accompaniment of the attached spiritual desires, the physical desires alone become an unreliable source for authenticity.

Both the spiritual and physical desires manifested within the conscience must always work together as a team in achieving the evidence necessary for identifying true conversion (i.e. true saving faith).

None at All

I also want to point out *the EUCs* can only effectively identify false regeneration (i.e. false conversion) with individuals who do not exhibit *any* of the three specific EUCs — reading, praying, and sharing — after they confess conversion. It is only these *none-at-all* individuals that *Desires: Characteristics of True Conversion* is specifically targeted to reach with this information found in the Word of God, as outlined in the EUCs.

The Sheep and Goats

I think we can learn from Christ's Parable of the Weeds in Matthew 13:24-30 and how Satan works to deceive the Body of Christ by mingling his (Satan's) children with God's Children (Rom. 8:16), often making it very difficult for authentic believers to discern between the true sheep from the goats (Mt. 25:32-33). That is why it so important for the Body of Christ to read and study the Word of God: the more familiar we are with God's

Word, the easier it will be for us in detecting the false converts in order to share the truth of the Gospel of Jesus Christ and the EUCs as outlined in this book with them (Ro. 8:9; 2 Ti. 3:16-17; 1 Jn. 2:5).

Terminologies

At this juncture, I think it would be important for me to define some words and terminologies used in *Desires: Characteristics of True Conversion.* The words *cause, method, and effect* and their terminologies are as follows:

CAUSE: The cause of true conversion is a sovereign work of God the Holy Spirit and is identified in Scripture as regeneration. More specifically, regeneration is the cause or the root of true conversion, and true conversion is the effect or the fruit of regeneration.

METHOD: The method is the procedure prescribed in Scripture that involves submitting to the work of the Holy Spirit, repenting of our sins, and coming to God through the saving knowledge of His One and Only Son, Jesus Christ, Who is the only mediator between God and men.

EFFECT: The effect is a change in our character, attitude, emotion, and viewpoint from one of indifference, disbelief, and antagonism to one of acceptance, belief, and enthusiastic support for the Father, Son, and Holy Spirit and the teachings and precepts found within the Holy Bible.

One Factor

The single factor in uniting the cause, method, and effects of the EUCs of true conversion — according to the Holy Bible — is *regeneration.* If I could use just one word to describe my book

Desires: Characteristics of True Conversion, it would be the word *regeneration.* We will explore and identify the origin and the cause of regeneration from a correct Biblical perspective so that we can understand the importance of identifying true conversion at a personal level. Let us explore and identify the *cause, method, and effects* of authentic conversion as we study the three *Essential Universal Characteristics (EUCs)* of true conversion so you can better determine for yourself if you are — in fact — a truly converted sinner, trusting in Christ alone for your salvation. Below is a chart of the *Process of Authentic Conversion* to help you better understand the *cause, method, and effects* of authentic conversion and its process from a correct Biblical perspective.

The Process of Authentic Conversion

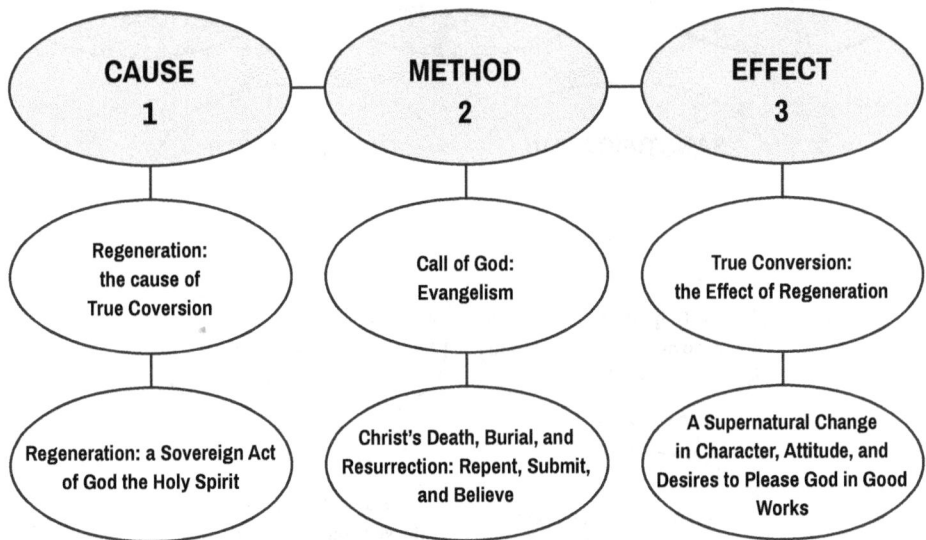

CAUSE 1	METHOD 2	EFFECT 3
Regeneration: the cause of True Coversion	Call of God: Evangelism	True Conversion: the Effect of Regeneration
Regeneration: a Sovereign Act of God the Holy Spirit	Christ's Death, Burial, and Resurrection: Repent, Submit, and Believe	A Supernatural Change in Character, Attitude, and Desires to Please God in Good Works

The stages in the salvation process from a Reformed view are as follows:

1. Election, foreknowledge, redemption, regeneration, justification, sanctification, and glorification (Ro. 8:29-30).

Below is a chart that explains the process of salvation from a Reformed perspective:

The Reformed Order of Salvation

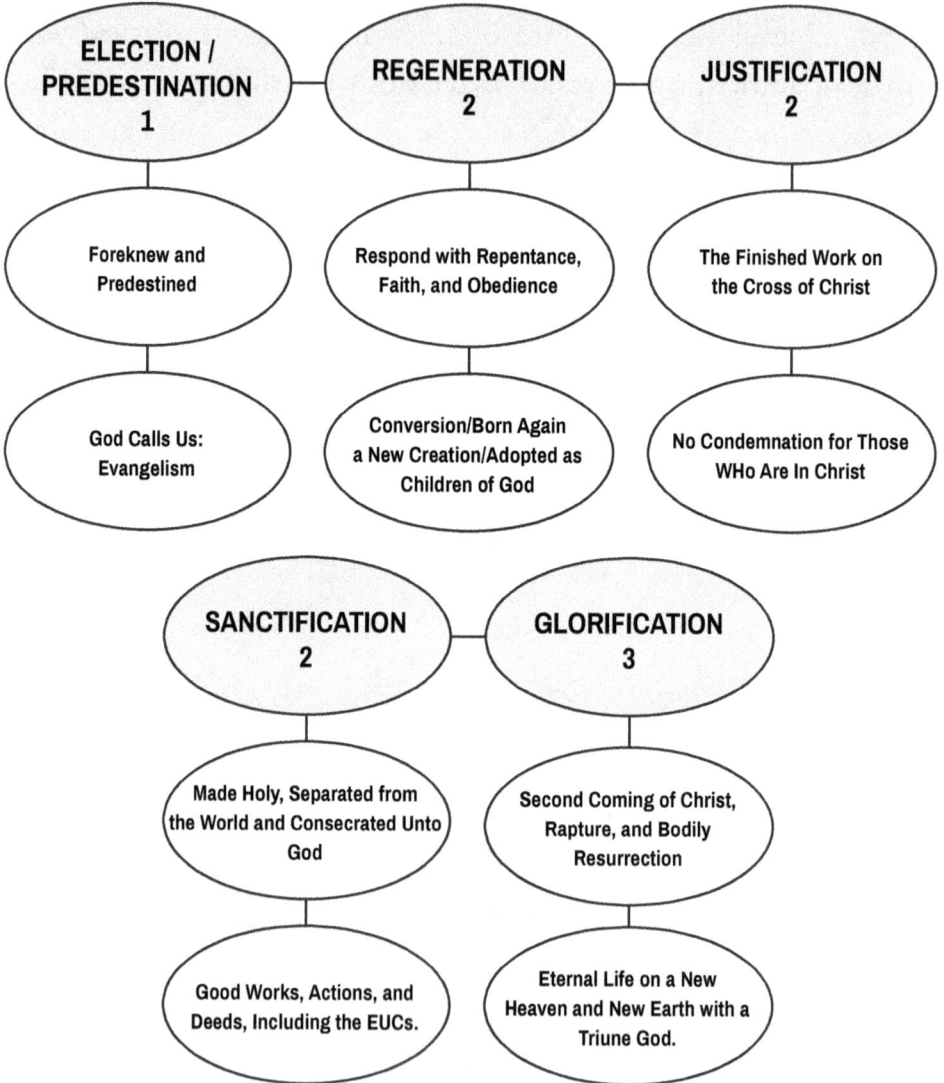

ELECTION / PREDESTINATION
1

Foreknew and Predestined

God Calls Us: Evangelism

REGENERATION
2

Respond with Repentance, Faith, and Obedience

Conversion/Born Again a New Creation/Adopted as Children of God

JUSTIFICATION
2

The Finished Work on the Cross of Christ

No Condemnation for Those WHo Are In Christ

SANCTIFICATION
2

Made Holy, Separated from the World and Consecrated Unto God

Good Works, Actions, and Deeds, Including the EUCs.

GLORIFICATION
3

Second Coming of Christ, Rapture, and Bodily Resurrection

Eternal Life on a New Heaven and New Earth with a Triune God.

The Election

God calls His elect when He draws them unto Christ at the moment of regeneration, which precedes the call of the elect unto repentance (Mk. 1:14-15; Ac. 2:38, 3:19, 5:31, 17:30; 2 Ti. 2:25; He. 9:15). When God the Holy Spirit produces within the elect regeneration (Ez. 36:26; Jn. 3:5-8; 2 Co. 5:17; Tit. 3:5;), He gives the adopted child of God the ability to now comprehend their need for Jesus Christ (i.e. a Savior) and to respond appropriately to Him with repentance, faith, and obedience. This means that in the Reformed view, regeneration precedes faith and repentance, but not in the Arminian view. In the Reformed view, before the Supernatural Divine call of God is *His Decree of Election.* The Arminian view has God's Decree of Election occurring after *evangelism* and *faith.* Election is the act of God choosing all who would be saved, even before time existed and before the foundation of the earth (Mt. 25:34; Ep. 1:4-6, 11; 2 Ti. 1:9; He. 4:3; 1 Pe. 1:20). The Apostle Paul tells us in the book of Romans that God foreknew certain people and predestined them to be conformed to the image of His Son, Jesus Christ[2]. Paul also said in verse 30 that those who are called are justified. When God calls us, we are immediately regenerated, and we turn away from our sin in repentance to God, and at that same moment, we become justified. Those who are justified are immediately glorified, in the sense that we have been adopted as children of God. We read in Romans 8:29-30 these words:

> "[29]*For those God foreknew, He also predestined to be conformed to the image of His Son, so that He would be the firstborn among many brothers.* [30]*And those He predestined, He*

---

2   Sproul, R. C. (1986). Chosen by God. Wheaton, IL: Tyndale House Publishers.

*also called; those He called, He also justified; those He justi-
fied, He also glorified."*

Here are more Scriptures for further study: Jn. 6:70, 15:16;
Ro. 8:18-28, 33; Ep. 1:3-11, 2:8-9; Col. 3:12; 1 Th. 1:4; 2 Th.
2:13; 2 Ti. 2:10; 1 Pe. 1:1-2.

In the Arminian view, the order of salvation is as follows: evangelism, followed by faith, election, repentance, regeneration, justification, perseverance, and glorification. These differences may
have various other specific distinctions that are not mentioned
here, but in a general sense, this comparison shows the basic differences between the two systems.

I think the determining factor regarding which view we will
adhere to, either Calvinism or Arminianism, is completely contingent upon our view of the sovereignty of God (Ep. 1:11). Is God
fully sovereign, or is He partially sovereign?

Act of God

In regeneration, God allows, tolerates, and authorizes the new
spiritual life within each follower through Christ, raising him or
her from a spiritual death and giving him or her *now* the *ability*
and *capacity* to be able to repent and trust in Jesus Christ as he or
she becomes a new creation (Tit. 3:5; Mt. 19:28). Unless we sub-
mit to God and come to Him on His terms and conditions (i.e.
being born again), we will never see the result (i.e. Heaven). Without regeneration, there can be no justification, sanctification, or
glorification (i.e. salvation).

"I believe that the work of regeneration, conversion, sanctification, and faith, is not an act of man's free will and power, but of
the mighty, efficacious and irresistible grace of God." — Charles
Spurgeon.

"So difficult is our salvation that only GOD can make it possible." — Paul Washer.

"Regeneration is something that is accomplished by God. A dead man cannot raise himself from the dead." — R.C. Sproul.

The Process

Because regeneration is a sovereign work of God the Holy Spirit, those who are once-and-for-all regenerated have a new heart, soul, and spirit created, and embedded within their conscience supernaturally, which means that God the Holy Spirit brings people — through His saving grace — a regenerated and transformed new life, even though they were previously in a state of rebellion and separation from Him (Jn. 3:3-8; Ep. 2:5; Tit. 3:5). Scripture tells us that all people are born "dead in sins and trespasses" (Ep. 2:1). Because of our sinful nature, we are unable to do anything that would be considered pleasing to God. Nobody can naturally seek after God without God's gift of regeneration (Ro. 3:10-11). That is because the sinful nature of men and women is completely unable to perceive or understand the things of God, without regeneration by God the Holy Spirit (Jn. 3:3; Ro. 8:6-8; 1 Co. 2:14). It is because of our sinful nature we are unable to understand or perceive even the *reason* for the need to trust in Christ. Apart from the work of God's saving grace — specifically referred to as regeneration — we simply cannot even comprehend the reason we need Christ.

Five Precepts

In regeneration, God re-creates supernaturally a new conscience and heart (i.e. mind, soul, and spirit) — which include newly restored and reborn will, emotions, devotion, love, and *desires* in the child of God to enable him or her to live life in such a way that glorifies and pleases God, through the implementation and manifestation of our good words, deeds, and actions, including the EUCs. It is these supernatural changes that are newly implanted by God deep within our conscience that we identify as *desires (i.e. our new will)* to obey God which precedes the physical manifestation of our good works, deeds, and actions, that cannot be conjured up by just an intellectual understanding of God and Jesus but are completely a sovereign act of the Triune God. It is these *desires* that we will be focusing on in *Desires: Characteristics of True Conversion*, which are based on five Biblical precepts. The five Biblical precepts are as follows:

1. Regeneration is the sovereign act of the Triune God.
2. Regeneration is the cause of true conversion.
3. True conversion is the effect of regeneration.
4. The absence of regeneration is the absence of the work of the Triune God.
5. The absence of the work of the Triune God is the nullification of justification, sanctification, and glorification (i.e. true conversion).

The logical conclusion of these five precepts mentioned above is that true regeneration precedes and produces and is the cause and effect of true conversion. Let me explain this to you in a different way:

- Regeneration: is a sovereign work of the Triune God.
- Regeneration + Triune God = application of the EUCs (i.e. true conversion).
- No regeneration: The Triune God is not involved.
- No regeneration – Triune God = no application of the EUCs (i.e. false conversion).

Corresponding Actions

Distinguishing between true and false conversions is completely and absolutely contingent upon the evidence of the Holy Spirit-caused and Holy Spirit-powered desires that precede the physical manifestation of the good works of our faith, as they are revealed to us in the Word of God and the EUCs. Genuine faith will always be accompanied by corresponding actions that are consistent with the essential precepts and teachings of the Christian faith as outlined in Scripture and the EUCs. Simply professing our faith verbally *only* without demonstrating our faith through the outward physical manifestation of good works, deeds, and actions, primarily the three EUCs, is not referred to in Scripture as just an incomplete and ineffective faith but is actually identified as being a dead faith (Ja. 2:14, 26).

The Interconnection

The Apostle James argues that an authentic faith must produce good works or deeds; otherwise, it is a dead faith. That is because works and saving faith are interconnected in the Biblical Christian worldview: they cannot be separated from this authentic Biblical precept. The interconnection of faith and works is absolutely an evidential proof of a sincere, living, and authentic faith, not a dead one. A dead faith has none of the specific EUCs attached to it, such as the Holy Spirit-caused and Holy Spirit-driven *desires* to read, pray, and share your faith (Mt. 28:18-20; Ph. 4:6; 1 Th. 5:17; 1 Tim. 4:13; 2 Ti. 3:16-17).

Identifying the Difference

This book, *Desires: Characteristics of True Conversion,* as mentioned previously, is not a book specifically about good works in and of themselves but is about having the supernatural desires that precede our good works, deeds, and actions which is the only way to honestly and accurately identify the difference between true and false conversion at a personal level. Not only do we need to pay attention to the physical manifestation of our good works, which are the byproducts and indicators of saving faith, but we also need to first and foremost, pay attention to the identity of the spiritual reality of the actual *desires* which precede our good works that were implanted deep within our conscience by God the Holy Spirit at the moment of our regeneration and justification. It is through the evidence of the physical manifestation of good works and the application of the preceding desires which include the three EUCs, initiated and caused by the Holy Spirit, identified within the Christian life, that the personal proof of authentic and true conversion exists. In other words, *"No good works manifested; no saving faith observed."* I will show you how to Biblically identify and understand the evidence of true conversion through just three Essential Universal Characteristics (EUCs) for you to recognize if — in fact — you are authentically converted.

Validation

I now want to show you briefly how *Desires: Characteristics of True Conversion* and its EUCs are substantiated through Scripture. The reason I must validate the principles and precepts of the EUCs from Scripture is that the Holy Bible must always be the *Final Court of Arbitration.* In other words, if the Word of God does not support the teaching in this book, *Desires: Characteristics of True Conversion,* and its EUCs, then they must be discarded.

Supporting Principles

Many verses in Scripture support the principles of the EUCs, and I will not have the time or the space to go through all of them with you in this book, but I will go through the main verses with you. I want to encourage you to do further study on your own on the EUCs topic after you have completed reading this book. The reason why I have selected both the Book of James, and the Book of Ephesians is that I have heard people make comments over the years that these two books are contradictory. This false accusation is a misunderstanding of the context of the passages in question. Let me briefly explain: James is referring to a type or kind of faith, and Paul is talking about the cause of faith. They do not contradict, but instead, they complement one another. I do believe that the Book of James alone will give us enough Scriptural support to validate the premise of *Desires: Characteristics of True Conversion* and its EUCs. We will start with the Book of James. Let's begin!

The Context

The context the Apostle James is using in his teaching in chapter two is that the evidence of our salvation is personally identified by the kind of faith that produces good works — not by faith that does not produce good works. In James 2:14, James tells us here, *"14What good is it, my brothers, if someone claims to have faith, but has no deeds? Can such faith save him?"* This is a rhetorical question, and the answer to this question is obviously no!

Then James again tells us in verse 17 that if faith has no action, then that faith is dead.

"17So too, faith by itself, if it does not result in action, is dead." Then James goes on to say this about faith in verses 18-19: *"18But*

someone will say, 'You have faith, and I have deeds.' Show me your faith without deeds, and I will show you my faith by my deeds. [19]You believe that God is one. Good for you! Even the demons believe that—and shudder." Then in James 2:26, he tells us, *"...faith without works is dead."* James confirms that deeds (or actions) are byproducts and indicators of true conversion. James compares faith without works to a dead body without a spirit. He says that *"For as the body apart from the spirit is dead, so also faith apart from works is dead"* (Ja. 2:26). It is the works, deeds, and actions that are the byproducts and indicators of true conversion. That is exactly what I am trying to communicate to the reader in my book, *Desires: Characteristics of True Conversion,* which is about the Supernatural desires found deep within the conscience which precede the good works that are implanted into the convert's heart and mind at the moment of regeneration and justification by God the Holy Spirit (Tit. 3:1-8).

Byproducts and Indicators

What I am trying to help the reader understand is that good deeds in and of themselves do not justify us or make us righteous before God, nor are they the means to salvation; but good deeds, works, and actions are byproducts and indicators, which are the evidence of true conversion. In other words, true conversion is not caused by good works, but good works are caused by true conversion. You must personally look at yourself to see if you have Supernatural *desires* that are found deep within your conscience which precede your good works, deeds, and actions. Due to this EUC discovery, we can now recognize and identify the authenticity of our conversion at a personal level, simply by observing the deep spiritual desires found within our conscience that precede the outward physical manifestation of our good works in our everyday life. The passages mentioned below validate the premise of the EUCs — all by themselves — beyond all reasonable doubt.

Overviews

1. EUCs and the Book of James Overview

James's teaching is absolutely consistent with the premise of the EUCs.

- The EUC premise: The absence of the Holy Spirit-driven *desires* (i.e. EUCs) within the self-professing regenerated follower of Christ's conscience is synonymous with the absence of God the Holy Spirit and authentic regeneration, meaning the person has a false conversion.
- The Biblical proof text: *"For as the body apart from the spirit is dead, so also faith apart from works is dead" (Ja. 2:26). "What good is it, my brothers, if someone claims to have faith, but has no deeds? Can such faith save him?" (Ja. 2:14).*

2. EUCs and the Book of Ephesians Overview

The teachings in the Book of Ephesians are absolutely consistent with the premise of the EUCs.

The EUC premise: Good works are byproducts and indicators of true conversion. Regeneration is the sovereign act of God the Holy Spirit and is the cause and effect of true conversion. Paul is saying in Ephesians 2:8-9, we are not saved by good works. Salvation is a gift from God that cannot be earned, not even through our good works. The absence of the most essential good works — specifically the EUCs — is the absence of God the Holy Spirit.

The absence of God the Holy Spirit is the absence of justification, sanctification, and glorification (i.e. true conversion).

- The Biblical proof text: *"It is by grace you have been saved through faith, and this not from yourselves; it is the gift of God, not by works, so that no one can boast" (Ep. 2: 8-9).*

3. EUCs and the Book of Titus Overview #1

Paul's teaching in the Book of Titus is absolutely consistent with the premise of the EUCs.

The EUC premise: The absence of the Holy Spirit-driven *desires* (i.e. EUCs) within the regenerated follower of Christ's conscience is synonymous with the absence of God the Holy Spirit and authentic regeneration, meaning the person has a false conversion. The *Essential Universal Characteristics (EUCs)* are three desires that spiritually precede the physical manifestation of our good works, which have been supernaturally implanted deep within our conscience (i.e. heart, mind, and soul) by God the Holy Spirit at the moment of regeneration and justification.

- The Biblical proof text:

"⁵He saved us, not by the righteous deeds we had done, but according to His mercy, through the washing of new birth and renewal by the Holy Spirit. ⁶This is the Spirit He poured out on us abundantly through Jesus Christ our Savior, ⁷so that, having been justified by His grace, we would become heirs with the hope of eternal life. ⁸This saying is trustworthy. And I want you to emphasize these things, so that those who have believed God will take care to devote themselves to good deeds. These things are excellent and profitable for the people" (Tit. 3:5-8).

4. EUCs and the Book of 1 John 2:3-4 Overview

The teaching in the Book of 1 John 2:3-4 is absolutely consistent with the premise of the EUCs.

- The EUC premise: The absence of the Holy Spirit-driven *desires* (i.e. EUCs) within the regenerated follower of Christ's conscience is synonymous with the absence of God the Holy Spirit and authentic regeneration, meaning the person has a false conversion.
- The Biblical proof text:

"³By this we can be sure that we have come to know Him: if we keep His commandments. ⁴If anyone says, "I know Him," but does not keep His commandments, he is a liar, and the truth is not in him" (1 Jn. 2:3-4).

5. EUCs and the Book of John Overview

John's teaching is absolutely consistent with the premise of the EUCs.

- The EUC premise: The absence of the Holy Spirit-driven *desires* (i.e. EUCs) within the regenerated follower of Christ's conscience is synonymous with the absence of God the Holy Spirit and authentic regeneration, meaning the person has a false conversion.
- The Biblical proof text: *"If you love Me, you will keep My commandments" (Jn. 14:15).*

6. EUCs and the Book of Titus Overview #2

Paul's teaching in the Book of Titus is absolutely consistent with the premise of the EUCs.

The EUC premise: The evidence of our true conversion is that we have desires that spiritually precede the physical manifestation of our good works. These desires have been supernaturally implanted deep within our conscience (i.e. heart, mind, and soul) by God the Holy Spirit at the moment of regeneration and justification.

The Biblical proof text:

"⁵He saved us, not by the righteous deeds we had done, but according to His mercy, through the washing of new birth and renewal by the Holy Spirit. ⁶This is the Spirit He poured out on us abundantly through Jesus Christ our Savior, ⁷so that, having been justified by His grace, we would become heirs with the hope of eternal life. ⁸This saying is trustworthy. And I want you to emphasize these things, so that those who have believed God will take care to devote themselves to good deeds. These things are excellent and profitable for the people" (Tit. 3:5-8).

7. EUCs and the Book of Titus Overview #3

Paul's teaching in the Book of Titus is absolutely consistent with the premise of the EUCs.

The EUC premise: Good deeds do not justify us or make us righteous before God, nor are they the means to salvation; but good deeds and actions are byproducts and indicators, which are the evidence of true conversion. In other words, true conversion is not caused by good works, but good works is caused by true conversion.

The Biblical proof text:

"⁵He saved us, not by the righteous deeds we had done, but according to His mercy, through the washing of new birth and renewal by the Holy Spirit. ⁶This is the Spirit He poured out

on us abundantly through Jesus Christ our Savior, ⁷so that, having been justified by His grace, we would become heirs with the hope of eternal life. ⁸This saying is trustworthy. And I want you to emphasize these things, so that those who have believed God will take care to devote themselves to good deeds. These things are excellent and profitable for the people" (Tit. 3:5-8).

Chapter One

Essential Universal Characteristics
READ

Reading the Word of God

Studying to Show Yourself Approved

According to the *State of the Bible USA 2024* survey conducted by the American Bible Society, Bible owners were asked, "how often they read the Bible outside of a church service." Not surprisingly, only 10% of respondents said they do so every day; a shocking 40% never touch their Bibles outside of a church service! For the full report, please read the document, *State of the Bible USA 2024*[3].

These *State of the Bible USA 2024* survey statistics do not surprise me and are absolutely consistent with the premise of the EUCs. Let me ask you six questions that all have the word "yes" attached as their answers.

1. Is the Bible the only Divinely inspired written recorded Word of God in existence?
2. Is the Bible the primary way that God communicates His thoughts and His will to people?

3. Is prayer the primary way that people communicate their needs and desires to God?

4. Does the Bible reveal God's creation, provision, judgment, deliverance, covenant, and promises?

5. Does the Bible explain the original plan of God, how it was corrupted, and how God has provided for man's restoration through His Son, Jesus Christ?

6. Does the Bible command believers to share the Gospel of Jesus Christ to a lost and dying world?

Let me ask you two more questions. **1.**) If we believe the above six questions about the Bible are true, then why do we see that only 10% of self-professing Christians in America read their Bibles daily outside of church services; and **2.**) Why do only 40% of self-professing Christians in America say they never touch their Bibles outside of church services?

The Answer in the EUCs

One of the premises of the EUCs is that authentic conversions can be positively identified through reading the Bible daily, which is an authentic regeneration indicator. By simply reversing the statistics found in the *State of the Bible 2024* survey that was recently conducted by the American Bible Society, we can with good reason and with a high probability in accuracy argue that the conclusive data discovered in the *State of the Bible 2024* survey is consistent and compatible with the premise of this book, *Desires: Characteristics of True Conversion*. Let me explain. Taken together, *The State of the Bible 2024* survey's conclusions that 90% of self-professing Christians in America do not read their Bibles outside of church service and only 60% of self-professing Christians in America actually touch their Bibles outside of a church service are completely compatible with at least one of the most important premises in my book:

1. *The absence of the number one Essential Universal Characteristic — reading the Bible — is clearly irrefutable evidence of the absence of God the Holy Spirit in the life of a self-professing Christian in America.*

2. True conversion is the *effect* of an authentic regeneration, and regeneration is its *cause*. The lack of the physical manifestation of the Holy Spirit-caused *desire* to read the Bible shows that the absence of an authentic regeneration has been positively identified, meaning the person has a false conversion.

Even though the *State of the Bible 2024* survey only directly mentions the reading "of the Bible outside of a church service," we can logically assume that those same church members who are not interested in reading their Bibles are probably also not interested in praying to God and sharing their faith either.

The facts are in, and the results are clear. This can only reasonably mean one thing, solely based on the conclusive data generated from the *State of the Bible 2024* survey by the American Bible Society. These survey results are an absolute indicator of a high percentage of false conversions in the Church today! This is consistent with Bible prophecies of the *"End of the Age"* — specifically the great apostasy, also known as the *falling away* (Mt. 24:10-13; 1 Ti. 4:1-2). Let us see what the Bible has to say about the importance and benefits of reading God's Word.

What does Scripture say about the importance and benefits of reading the Word of God?

Matthew 4:4

"*4But Jesus answered, 'It is written: Man shall not live on bread alone, but on every word that comes from the mouth of God.'*"

2 Timothy 3:16-17

"*16All Scripture is God-breathed and is useful for instruction, for conviction, for correction, and for training in righteousness, 17so that the man of God may be complete, fully equipped for every good work.*"

John 17:17

"*17Sanctify them by the truth; Your word is truth.*"

2 Timothy 2:15

"*15Make every effort to present yourself approved to God, an unashamed workman who accurately handles the word of truth.*"

Acts 17 11

"*11Now the Bereans were more noble-minded than the Thessalonians, for they received the message with great eagerness and examined the Scriptures every day to see if these teachings were true.*"

Colossians 3:16-17

"*16Let the word of Christ richly dwell within you as you teach and admonish one another with all wisdom, and as you sing psalms, hymns, and spiritual songs with gratitude in your hearts to God. ¹⁷And whatever you do, in word or deed, do it all in the name of the Lord Jesus, giving thanks to God the Father through Him."*

Ephesians 6:17

"¹⁷And take the helmet of salvation and the sword of the Spirit, which is the word of God."

Hebrews 4:12

"¹²For the word of God is living and active. Sharper than any double-edged sword, it pierces even to dividing soul and spirit, joints and marrow. It judges the thoughts and intentions of the heart."

Isaiah 34:16

"¹⁶Search and read the scroll of the LORD: Not one of these will go missing, not one will lack her mate, because He has ordered it by His mouth, and He will gather them by His Spirit."

Job 23:12

"¹²I have not departed from the command of His lips; I have treasured the words of His mouth more than my daily bread."

John 6:63

"⁶³The Spirit gives life; the flesh profits nothing. The words I have spoken to you are spirit and they are life."

Luke 11:28

"²⁸But He replied, 'Blessed rather are those who hear the word of God and obey it.'"

Luke 24:44-45

"44Jesus said to them, 'These are the words I spoke to you while I was still with you: Everything must be fulfilled that is written about Me in the Law of Moses, the Prophets, and the Psalms.' 45Then He opened their minds to understand the Scriptures."

Psalms 12:6

"6The words of the LORD are flawless, like silver refined in a furnace, like gold purified sevenfold."

Revelation 1:2

"2who testifies to everything he saw. This is the word of God and the testimony of Jesus Christ."

Revelation 22:19

"19And if anyone takes away from the words of this book of prophecy, God will take away his share in the tree of life and the holy city, which are described in this book."

1 Peter 1:25

"25but the word of the Lord stands forever. And this is the word that was proclaimed to you."

1 Thessalonians 2:13

"13And we continually thank God because, when you received the word of God that you heard from us, you accepted it not as the word of men, but as the true word of God—the word which is now at work in you who believe."

2 Peter 3:16

"16He writes this way in all his letters, speaking in them about such matters. Some parts of his letters are hard to understand, *which ignorant and unstable people distort, as they do the rest of the Scriptures, to their own destruction."*

Romans 15:4

"⁴For everything that was written in the past was written for our instruction, so that through endurance and the encouragement of the Scriptures, we might have hope."

Mark 13:31

"³¹Heaven and earth will pass away, but My words will never pass away."

John 1:1

"¹In the beginning was the Word, and the Word was with God, and the Word was God."

Psalms 119:105

"¹⁰⁵Your word is a lamp to my feet and a light to my path."

Psalms 119:11

"¹¹I have hidden Your word in my heart that I might not sin against You."

Psalms 1:1-6

"¹Blessed is the man who does not walk in the counsel of the wicked, or set foot on the path of sinners, or sit in the seat of mockers. ²But his delight is in the Law of the LORD, and on His law he meditates day and night. ³He is like a tree planted by streams of water, yielding its fruit in season, whose leaf does not wither, and who prospers in all he does. ⁴Not so the wicked! For they are like chaff driven off by the wind. ⁵Therefore the

wicked will not stand in the judgment, nor sinners in the assembly of the righteous. 6For the LORD guards the path of the righteous, but the way of the wicked will perish."

Proverbs 30:5

"5Every word of God is flawless; He is a shield to those who take refuge in Him."

Isaiah 40:8

"8The grass withers and the flowers fall, but the word of our God stands forever."

Chapter Two

Essential Universal Characteristics
PRAY

Communicating with God

Praying Without Ceasing

Prayer is the primary method of communication by humans to God; but according to the Pew Research Center[4] only 60% of Christians pray daily, 17% pray weekly, 5% pray monthly, 9% pray seldom or never, and 1% of Christian adults do not know if they pray.

The reason Christians pray is that God commands us to *"¹⁶Rejoice always, ¹⁷pray without ceasing, ¹⁸give thanks in all circumstances; for this is the will of God in Christ Jesus for you"* (1 Th. 5:16-18 ESV).

What does Scripture say about prayer?

Philippians 4:6

> *"⁶Be anxious for nothing, but in everything, by prayer and petition, with thanksgiving, present your requests to God."*

---

4   The Pew Research Center, www.pewresearch.org. Frequency of Prayer – Religion in America.

Mark 11:24

"²⁴Therefore I tell you, whatever you ask for in prayer, believe that you have received it, and it will be yours."

Romans 8:26

"²⁶In the same way, the Spirit helps us in our weakness. For we do not know how we ought to pray, but the Spirit Himself intercedes for us with groans too deep for words."

Matthew 6:6

"⁶But when you pray, go into your inner room, shut your door, and pray to your Father, who is unseen. And your Father, who sees what is done in secret, will reward you."

Matthew 26:41

"⁴¹Watch and pray so that you will not enter into temptation. For the spirit is willing, but the body is weak."

1 Thessalonians 5:16-18

"¹⁶Rejoice at all times. ¹⁷Pray without ceasing. ¹⁸Give thanks in every circumstance, for this is God's will for you in Christ Jesus."

2 Chronicles 7:14

"¹⁴and if My people who are called by My name humble themselves and pray and seek My face and turn from their wicked ways, then I will hear from heaven, forgive their sin, and heal their land."

2 Chronicles 6:21

"21Hear the plea of Your servant and of Your people Israel when they pray toward this place. May You hear from heaven, Your dwelling place. May You hear and forgive."

1 Chronicles 16:11

"11Seek out the LORD and His strength; seek His face always."

Ephesians 6:18

"18Pray in the Spirit at all times, with every kind of prayer and petition. To this end, stay alert with all perseverance in your prayers for all the saints."

Jeremiah 29:12

"12Then you will call upon Me and come and pray to Me, and I will listen to you."

Job 22:27

"27You will pray to Him, and He will hear you, and you will fulfill your vows."

James 5:13

"13Is any one of you suffering? He should pray. Is anyone cheerful? He should sing praises."

Mark 11:24

"24Therefore I tell you, whatever you ask for in prayer, believe that you have received it, and it will be yours."

1 John 5:14-16

"14And this is the confidence that we have before Him: If we ask anything according to His will, He hears us. 15And if we know that He hears us in whatever we ask, we know that we already possess what we have asked of Him. 16If anyone sees his brother committing a sin not leading to death, he should ask God, who will give life to those who commit this kind of sin. There is a sin that leads to death; I am not saying he should ask regarding that sin."

Matthew 5:44

"44But I tell you, love your enemies and pray for those who persecute you,"

Matthew 26:41

"41Watch and pray so that you will not enter into temptation. For the spirit is willing, but the body is weak."

Proverbs 15:8

"8The sacrifice of the wicked is detestable to the LORD, but the prayer of the upright is His delight."

Psalms 17:6

"6I call on You, O God, for You will answer me. Incline Your ear to me; hear my words."

Psalm 102:17

"17He will turn toward the prayer of the destitute; He will not despise their prayer."

Psalms 141:2

"2May my prayer be set before You like incense, my uplifted hands like the evening offering."

Romans 12:2

"2Do not be conformed to this world, but be transformed by the renewing of your mind. Then you will be able to test and approve what is the good, pleasing, and perfect will of God."

Romans 12:12

"12Be joyful in hope, patient in affliction, persistent in prayer."

Psalms 4:1

"1Answer me when I call, O God of my righteousness! You have relieved my distress; show me grace and hear my prayer."

Luke 11:2-4

"2So Jesus told them, 'When you pray, say: "Father, hallowed be Your name. Your kingdom come. 3Give us each day our daily bread. 4And forgive us our sins, for we also forgive everyone who sins against us. And lead us not into temptation."'"

Luke 6:12

"12In those days Jesus went out to the mountain to pray, and He spent the night in prayer to God."

Luke 18:1

"1Then Jesus told them a parable about their need to pray at all times and not lose heart:"

Colossians 4:2

"*²Devote yourselves to prayer, being watchful and thankful,*"

1 Timothy 2:8

"*⁸Therefore I want the men everywhere to pray, lifting up holy hands, without anger or dissension.*"

James 4:3

"*³And when you do ask, you do not receive, because you ask with wrong motives, that you may squander it on your pleasures.*"

James 5:16-17

"*¹⁶Therefore confess your sins to each other and pray for each other so that you may be healed. The prayer of a righteous man has great power to prevail.*"

1 John 1:9

"*⁹If we confess our sins, He is faithful and just to forgive us our sins and to cleanse us from all unrighteousness.*

Chapter Three

Essential Universal Characteristics
SHARE

Sharing Your Faith

Being Unashamed of the Gospel

Statistics show that approximately 95% of all Christians have never won a soul to Christ, 80% of all Christians do not consistently witness for Christ, less than 2% of Christians are involved in the ministry of evangelism, and 71% percent of Christians do not give toward the financing of the Great Commission[5].

Below I want to share with you Bible verses about evangelism. These Bible verses will equip you with knowledge and provide you with inspiration to share your faith with grace, wisdom, and love — and do not forget to sprinkle them with gentleness and respect. These verses below are to help guide you and provide a deeper understanding of how God wants us to share our faith with others.

What does Scripture say about sharing your faith?

---

[5] "*Street Level Evangelism: Where is the Space for the Local Evangelist,*" by Michael Parrott, Acts Evangelism, Spokane, WA. 1993, pp. 9-11.

Psalms 105:1

"¹Give thanks to the LORD, call upon His name; make known His deeds among the nations."

Proverbs 11:30

"³⁰The fruit of the righteous is a tree of life, and he who wins souls is wise."

Isaiah 6:8

"⁸Then I heard the voice of the Lord saying: 'Whom shall I send? Who will go for us?'"

Isaiah 12:4

"⁴and on that day you will say: 'Give praise to the LORD; proclaim His name! Make His works known among the peoples; declare that His name is exalted.'"

Isaiah 45:22

"²²Turn to Me and be saved, all the ends of the earth; for I am God, and there is no other."

Ezekiel 3:16-19

"¹⁶At the end of seven days the word of the LORD came to me, saying, ¹⁷'Son of man, I have made you a watchman for the house of Israel. Whenever you hear a word from My mouth, give them a warning from Me. ¹⁸If I say to the wicked man, "You will surely die," but you do not warn him or speak out to warn him from his wicked way to save his life, that wicked man will die in his iniquity, and I will hold you responsible for his blood.'"

Ezekiel 38:23

"*23I will magnify and sanctify Myself, and will reveal Myself in the sight of many nations. Then they will know that I am the LORD.*"

Malachi 1:11

"*11For My name will be great among the nations, from where the sun rises to where it sets. In every place, incense and pure offerings will be presented in My name, because My name will be great among the nations,' says the LORD of Hosts.*"

Matthew 5:15-16

"*15Neither do people light a lamp and put it under a basket. Instead, they set it on a stand, and it gives light to everyone in the house. 16In the same way, let your light shine before men, that they may see your good deeds and glorify your Father in heaven.*"

Matthew 9:37-38

"*37Anyone who loves his father or mother more than Me is not worthy of Me; anyone who loves his son or daughter more than Me is not worthy of Me; 38and anyone who does not take up his cross and follow Me is not worthy of Me.*"

Matthew 11:28

"*28Come to Me, all you who are weary and burdened, and I will give you rest.*"

Matthew 28:18-20

"*18Then Jesus came to them and said, 'All authority in heaven and on earth has been given to Me. 19Therefore go and make* *disciples of all nations, baptizing them in the name of the Father, and of the Son, and of the Holy Spirit, ²⁰and teaching them to obey all that I have commanded you. And surely I am with you always, even to the end of the age.'"*

Mark 16:16

"¹⁶Whoever believes and is baptized will be saved, but whoever does not believe will be condemned."

Luke 12:8

"⁸I tell you, everyone who confesses Me before men, the Son of Man will also confess him before the angels of God."

Luke 12:11-12

"'¹¹When you are brought before synagogues, rulers, and authorities, do not worry about how to defend yourselves or what to say. ¹²For at that time the Holy Spirit will teach you what you should say.'"

John 3:16-18

"¹⁶For God so loved the world that He gave His one and only Son, that everyone who believes in Him shall not perish but have eternal life. ¹⁷For God did not send His Son into the world to condemn the world, but to save the world through Him. ¹⁸Whoever believes in Him is not condemned, but whoever does not believe has already been condemned, because he has not believed in the name of God's one and only Son."

John 13:35

"³⁵By this everyone will know that you are My disciples, if you love one another."

John 14:6-7

"⁶Jesus answered, 'I am the way and the truth and the life. No one comes to the Father except through Me. ⁷If you had known Me, you would know My Father as well. From now on you do know Him and have seen Him.'"

John 15:8

"⁸This is to My Father's glory, that you bear much fruit, proving yourselves to be My disciples."

Acts 1:8

"⁸But you will receive power when the Holy Spirit comes upon you, and you will be My witnesses in Jerusalem, and in all Judea and Samaria, and to the ends of the earth."

Acts 13:47

"⁴⁷For this is what the Lord has commanded us: "I have made you a light for the Gentiles, to bring salvation to the ends of the earth."

Acts 20:24

"²⁴But I consider my life of no value to me, if only I may finish my course and complete the ministry I have received from the Lord Jesus — the ministry of testifying to the good news of God's grace."

Romans 1:16

"¹⁶I am not ashamed of the gospel, because it is the power of God for salvation to everyone who believes, first to the Jew, then to the Greek."

Romans 6:23

"23For the wages of sin is death, but the gift of God is eternal life in Christ Jesus our Lord"

Romans 10:10-17

"10For with your heart you believe and are justified, and with your mouth you confess and are saved. 11It is just as the Scripture says: 'Anyone who believes in Him will never be put to shame.' 12For there is no difference between Jew and Greek: The same Lord is Lord of all, and gives richly to all who call on Him, 13for, 'Everyone who calls on the name of the Lord will be saved.' 14How then can they call on the One in whom they have not believed? And how can they believe in the One of whom they have not heard? And how can they hear without someone to preach? 15And how can they preach unless they are sent? As it is written: 'How beautiful are the feet of those who bring good news!' 16But not all of them welcomed the good news. For Isaiah says, 'Lord, who has believed our message?' 17Consequently, faith comes by hearing, and hearing by the word of Christ."

1 Corinthians 3:6-9

"6I planted the seed and Apollos watered it, but God made it grow. 7So neither he who plants nor he who waters is anything, but only God, who makes things grow. 8He who plants and he who waters are one in purpose, and each will be rewarded according to his own labor. 9For we are God's fellow workers; you are God's field, God's building."

1 Corinthians 2:1-2

"¹When I came to you, brothers, I did not come with eloquence or wisdom as I proclaimed to you the testimony about God. ²For I resolved to know nothing while I was with you except Jesus Christ and Him crucified."

1 Corinthians 9:19-23

"¹⁹Though I am free of obligation to anyone, I make myself a slave to everyone, to win as many as possible. ²⁰To the Jews I became like a Jew, to win the Jews. To those under the law I became like one under the law (though I myself am not under the law), to win those under the law. ²¹To those without the law I became like one without the law (though I am not outside the law of God but am under the law of Christ), to win those without the law. ²²To the weak I became weak, to win the weak. I have become all things to all people so that by all possible means I might save some. ²³I do all this for the sake of the gospel, so that I may share in its blessings."

1 Corinthians 16:7-9

"⁷For I do not want to see you now only in passing; I hope to spend some time with you, if the Lord permits. ⁸But I will stay in Ephesus until Pentecost, ⁹because a great door for effective work has opened to me, even though many oppose me."

2 Corinthians 5:20

"²⁰Therefore we are ambassadors for Christ, as though God were making His appeal through us. We implore you on behalf of Christ: Be reconciled to God."

Galatians 2:7-9

"⁷On the contrary, they saw that I had been entrusted to preach the gospel to the uncircumcised, just as Peter had been to the circumcised. ⁸For the One who was at work in Peter's apostleship to the circumcised was also at work in my apostleship to the Gentiles. ⁹And recognizing the grace that I had been given, James, Cephas, and John — those reputed to be pillars — gave me and Barnabas the right hand of fellowship, so that we should go to the Gentiles, and they to the circumcised."

Ephesians 2:8-9

"⁸For it is by grace you have been saved through faith, and this not from yourselves; it is the gift of God, ⁹not by works, so that no one can boast."

Colossians 1:28-29

"²⁸We proclaim Him, admonishing and teaching everyone with all wisdom, so that we may present everyone perfect in Christ. ²⁹To this end I also labor, striving with all His energy working powerfully within me."

Colossians 4:2-6

"²Devote yourselves to prayer, being watchful and thankful, ³as you pray also for us, that God may open to us a door for the word, so that we may proclaim the mystery of Christ, for which I am in chains. ⁴Pray that I may declare it clearly, as I should. ⁵Act wisely toward outsiders, redeeming the time. ⁶Let your speech always be gracious, seasoned with salt, so that you may know how to answer everyone."

1 Thessalonians 1:4-5

"⁴Brothers who are beloved by God, we know that He has chosen you, ⁵because our gospel came to you not only in word, but also in power, in the Holy Spirit, and with great conviction — just as you know we lived among you for your sake."

2 Timothy 1:8-9

"⁸So do not be ashamed of the testimony of our Lord, or of me, His prisoner. Instead, join me in suffering for the gospel by the power of God. ⁹He has saved us and called us to a holy calling, not because of our works, but by His own purpose and by the grace He granted us in Christ Jesus before time began."

2 Timothy 2:15

"¹⁵Make every effort to present yourself approved to God, an unashamed workman who accurately handles the word of truth."

2 Timothy 4:5

"⁵But you, be sober in all things, endure hardship, do the work of an evangelist, fulfill your ministry."

1 Peter 3:15

"¹⁵But in your hearts sanctify Christ as Lord. Always be prepared to give a defense to everyone who asks you the reason for the hope that is in you. But respond with gentleness and respect,"

2 Peter 3:9

"⁹The Lord is not slow in keeping His promise as some understand slowness, but is patient with you, not wanting anyone to perish but everyone to come to repentance."

Fruit of the Spirit TEST

(Galatians 5:22-23)

Select the fruits of the Spirit that honestly apply to you:

1. Love   **Yes** ☐   **No** ☐   **Seldom** ☐
2. Joy   **Yes** ☐   **No** ☐   **Seldom** ☐
3. Peace   **Yes** ☐   **No** ☐   **Seldom** ☐
4. Patience   **Yes** ☐   **No** ☐   **Seldom** ☐
5. Kindness   **Yes** ☐   **No** ☐   **Seldom** ☐
6. Goodness   **Yes** ☐   **No** ☐   **Seldom** ☐
7. Faithfulness   **Yes** ☐   **No** ☐   **Seldom** ☐
8. Gentleness   **Yes** ☐   **No** ☐   **Seldom** ☐
9. Self-control   **Yes** ☐   **No** ☐   **Seldom** ☐

"Against such things there is no law" (Ga. 5:23b).

The fruit of the Spirit is the effect of regeneration, not its cause. Some people teach that if we repent and believe in Jesus Christ, then the Holy Spirit will regenerate us. But it is actually the other way around. Regeneration precedes our faith. Do you experience the *desires* of the fruit of regeneration in your life?

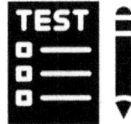

Works of the Flesh TEST

(Galatians 5:19-21)

Select the works of the flesh that honestly apply to you:

1. Sexual immorality	Yes ☐	No ☐	Seldom ☐
2. Impurity	Yes ☐	No ☐	Seldom ☐
3. Debauchery	Yes ☐	No ☐	Seldom ☐
4. Idolatry	Yes ☐	No ☐	Seldom ☐
5. Sorcery	Yes ☐	No ☐	Seldom ☐
6. Hatred	Yes ☐	No ☐	Seldom ☐
7. Discord	Yes ☐	No ☐	Seldom ☐
8. Jealousy	Yes ☐	No ☐	Seldom ☐
9. Rage	Yes ☐	No ☐	Seldom ☐
10. Rivalries	Yes ☐	No ☐	Seldom ☐
11. Divisions	Yes ☐	No ☐	Seldom ☐
12. Factions	Yes ☐	No ☐	Seldom ☐
13. Envy	Yes ☐	No ☐	Seldom ☐

14. Drunkenness	**Yes** ☐	**No** ☐	**Seldom** ☐
15. Orgies	**Yes** ☐	**No** ☐	**Seldom** ☐

"...I warn you,...those who practice such things will not inherit the kingdom of God" (Ga. 5:21).

Examine Yourself Test

Examine yourselves to see whether you are in the faith; test your-selves. Can't you see for yourselves that Jesus Christ is in you—unless you actually fail the test? (2 Co. 13:5)

1. Do you believe in Jesus Christ?
   Yes☐ No☐ Seldom☐

1 John 5:1 Everyone who believes that Jesus is the Christ is born of God, and everyone who loves the Father also loves the one born of Him.

1 John 5:13 I have written these things to you who believe in the name of the Son of God, so that you may know that you have eternal life.

2. Do you practice sin regularly?
   Yes☐ No☐ Seldom☐

1 John 3:9 Anyone born of God refuses to practice sin, because God's seed abides in him; he cannot go on sinning, because he has been born of God.

Romans 6:1 What then shall we say? Shall we continue in sin so that grace may increase?

Romans 6:2 By no means! How can we who died to sin live in it any longer?

3. Do you study God's Word daily?
Yes☐ **No**☐ **Seldom**☐

2 Timothy 2:15 Make every effort to present yourself approved to God, an unashamed workman who accurately handles the word of truth.

2 Timothy 3:16 All Scripture is God-breathed and is useful for instruction, for conviction, for correction, and for training in righteousness,

2 Timothy 3:17 so that the man of God may be complete, fully equipped for every good work.

4. Do you abide in Christ?
Yes☐ **No**☐ **Seldom**☐

John 15:4 Remain in Me, and I will remain in you. Just as no branch can bear fruit by itself unless it remains in the vine, neither can you bear fruit unless you remain in Me.

John 15:5 I am the vine and you are the branches. The one who remains in Me, and I in him, will bear much fruit. For apart from Me you can do nothing

5. Are you indifferent to sin?
Yes☐ **No**☐ **Seldom**☐

1 John 1:6 If we say we have fellowship with Him yet walk in the darkness, we lie and do not practice the truth.

1 John 1:7 But if we walk in the light as He is in the light, we have fellowship with one another, and the blood of Jesus His Son cleanses us from all sin.

1 John 1:8 If we say we have no sin, we deceive ourselves, and the truth is not in us.

6. Do you obey Christ?
Yes☐   No☐   Seldom☐

1 John 2:3 By this we can be sure that we have come to know Him: if we keep His commandments.

1 John 2:4 If anyone says, "I know Him," but does not keep His commandments, he is a liar, and the truth is not in him.

1 John 2:5 But if anyone keeps His word, the love of God has been truly perfected in him. By this we know that we are in Him:

1 John 2:6 Whoever claims to abide in Him must walk as Jesus walked.

7. Do you practice righteousness?
Yes☐   No☐   Seldom☐

1 John 3:7 Little children, let no one deceive you: The one who practices righteousness is righteous, just as Christ is righteous.

8. Do you pray for the lost?
Yes☐   No☐   Seldom☐

Matthew 9:37 Then He said to his disciples, "The harvest is plentiful, but the workers are few.

Matthew 9:38 Ask the Lord of the harvest, therefore, to send out workers into His harvest."

9. Do you go to church regularly?
Yes☐   No☐   Seldom☐

Hebrews 10:25 Let us not neglect meeting together, as some have made a habit, but let us encourage one another, and all the more as you see the Day approaching.

10. Do you pray to God daily?
Yes☐   No☐   Seldom☐

1 Thessalonians 5:17 Pray without ceasing.

1 Thessalonians 5:18 Give thanks in every circumstance, for this is God's will for you in Christ Jesus.

1 Timothy 2:8 Therefore I want the men everywhere to pray, lifting up holy hands, without anger or dissension.

11. Do you share the Gospel regularly?
Yes☐   No☐   Seldom☐

2 Timothy 1:8 So do not be ashamed of the testimony of our Lord, or of me, His prisoner. Instead, join me in suffering for the gospel by the power of God.

2 Timothy 1:9 He has saved us and called us with a holy calling, not because of our own works, but by His own purpose and by the grace He granted us in Christ Jesus before time eternal.

12. Do you keep yourself pure?
Yes☐   No☐   Seldom☐

1 John 5:18 We know that anyone born of God does not keep on sinning; the One who was born of God protects him, and the evil one cannot touch him.

13. Do you love your neighbor?
Yes☐   No☐   Seldom☐

Matthew 22:37 Jesus declared, "Love the Lord your God with all your heart and with all your soul and with all your mind. Matthew 22:38 This is the first and greatest commandment. Matthew 22:39 And the second is like it: 'Love your neighbor as yourself.'"

14. Do you believe that Jesus is God?
Yes☐   No☐   Seldom☐

John 1:1 In the beginning was the Word, and the Word was with God, and the Word was God.

Colossians 2:9 For in Christ all the fullness of the Deity dwells in bodily form.

15. Do you know and love Christ?
Yes☐   No☐   Seldom☐

John 14:15 If you love Me, you will keep My commandments.

1 John 2:3 By this we can be sure that we have come to know Him: if we keep His commandments.

1 John 2:4 If anyone says, "I know Him," but does not keep His commandments, he is a liar, and the truth is not in him.

1 John 2:5 But if anyone keeps His word, the love of God has been truly perfected in him. By this we know that we are in Him.

16. Do you worship God daily?
Yes☐   No☐   Seldom☐

Psalm 59:16 But I will sing of Your strength and proclaim Your loving devotion in the morning. For You are my fortress, my refuge in times of trouble.

Psalm 63:3 Because Your loving devotion is better than life, my lips will glorify You.

Psalm 63:4 So I will bless You as long as I live; in Your name I will lift my hands.

17. Do you desire to serve others?
Yes☐   No☐   Seldom☐

Galatians 5:13 For you, brothers, were called to freedom; but do not use your freedom as an opportunity for the flesh. Rather, serve one another in love.

Ephesians 6:7 Serve with good will, as to the Lord and not to men.

18. Do you love the things of this world?
Yes☐   No☐   Seldom☐

Titus 2:12 It instructs us to renounce ungodliness and worldly passions, and to live sensible, upright, and godly lives in the present age.

1 John 5:4 because everyone born of God overcomes the world. And this is the victory that has overcome the world: our faith.

1 John 5:5 Who then overcomes the world? Only he who believes that Jesus is the Son of God.

19. Do you love other Christians?
Yes☐   No☐   Seldom☐

1 John 3:14   We know that we have passed from death to life, because we love our brothers. The one who does not love remains in death.

John 13:34   A new commandment I give you: Love one another. As I have loved you, so also you must love one another.

John 13:35   By this all men will know that you are My disciples, if you love one another."

20. Do you forgive others?
Yes☐   No☐   Seldom☐

Mark 11:26   But if you do not forgive, neither will your Father in Heaven forgive your trespasses.

21. Do you enjoy reading your Bible?
Yes☐   No☐   Seldom☐

2 Timothy 3:16   All Scripture is God-breathed and is useful for instruction, for conviction, for correction, and for training in righteousness.

2 Timothy 3:17   so that the man of God may be complete, fully equipped for every good work.

22. Do you love God with all your heart, mind, soul, and strength?
Yes☐   No☐   Seldom☐

Mark 12:30   and you shall love the Lord your God with all your heart and with all your soul and with all your mind and with all your strength.

23. Do you desire to serve the Lord?
Yes☐　No☐　Seldom☐

Romans 12:11 Do not let your zeal subside; keep your spiritual fervor, serving the Lord.

24. Do you confess your sin?
Yes☐　No☐　Seldom☐

1 John 1:9 If we confess our sins, He is faithful and just to forgive us our sins and to cleanse us from all unrighteousness.

Romans 6:1 What then shall we say? Shall we continue in sin so that grace may increase?

Romans 6:2 By no means! How can we who died to sin live in it any longer?

25. Is your life dedicated to Jesus?
Yes☐　No☐　Seldom☐

Matthew 10:33 But whoever denies Me before men, I will also deny him before My Father in heaven.

Matthew 16:4 Then Jesus told His disciples, "If anyone would come after Me, he must deny himself and take up his cross and follow Me.

The Three Steps of Becoming a Christian

1. Repent.

Admit to God that you are a sinner. Repent, and turn away from your sin.

- Romans 3:23 *for all have sinned and fall short of the glory of God,*
- Romans 3:24 *and are justified by his grace as a gift, through the redemption that is in Christ Jesus.*
- Romans 6:23 *For the wages of sin is death, but the free gift of God is eternal life in Christ Jesus our Lord.*
- Acts 3:19 *Repent therefore, and turn again, that your sins may be blotted out.*
- 1 John 1:9 *If we confess our sins, He is faithful and just to forgive us our sins and to cleanse us from all unrighteousness.*

2. Believe.

Believe that Jesus Christ is God's Son and accept God's gift of forgiveness from sin.

- John 3:16 *For God so loved the world, that he gave his only Son, that whoever believes in him should not perish but have eternal life.*
- John 3:17 *For God did not send his Son into the world to condemn the world, but in order that the world might be saved through him.*
- John 3:18 *Whoever believes in him is not condemned, but whoever does not believe is condemned already, because he has not believed in the name of the only Son of God.*
- John 14:6 *Jesus said to him, "I am the way, and the truth, and the life. No one comes to the Father except through Me."*
- Act 4:12 *And there is salvation in no one else, for there is no other name under heaven given among men by which we must be saved.*
- Romans 5:8 *but God shows his love for us in that while we were still sinners, Christ died for us.*
- Ephesians 2:8 *For by grace you have been saved through faith. And this is not your own doing; it is the gift of God,*
- Ephesians 2:9 *not a result of works, so that no one may boast.*
- John 1:11 *He came to his own, and his own people did not receive him.*
- John 1:12 *But to all who did receive him, who believed in his name, he gave the right to become children of God,*
- John 1:13 *who were born, not of blood nor of the will of the flesh nor of the will of man, but of God.*

3. Confess.

Confess your faith in Jesus Christ as Savior and Lord.

- Romans 10:9 *because, if you confess with your mouth that* Jesus is Lord and believe in your heart that God raised him from the dead, you will be saved.
- Romans 10:10 *For with the heart one believes and is justified, and with the mouth one confesses and is saved.*
- Romans 10:13 *For "everyone who calls on the name of the Lord will be saved."*

Conclusion

In Mathew 7:21-23, when Jesus was preaching to His followers at the end of His Sermon on the Mount, Jesus said,

> ²¹*"Not everyone who says to Me, 'Lord, Lord,' will enter the kingdom of heaven, but only he who does the will of My Father in heaven. ²²Many will say to Me on that day, 'Lord, Lord, did we not prophesy in Your name, and in Your name drive out demons and perform many miracles?' ²³Then I will tell them plainly, 'I never knew you; depart from Me, you workers of lawlessness!'"*

This passage is not referring to the children of God who have received an authentic regeneration and have a genuine obedient relationship with the Father through Jesus Christ. This verse is obviously referring to the children of wrath, self-professors who associate themselves with the Christian body, who never had a personal, obedient, and committed relationship with Jesus Christ. When Jesus said, "I never knew you," Christ meant that He did not recognize these self-professing followers as true disciples, or even friends, and that those who will say to Jesus, "Lord, Lord...," on the day of judgment, will not have come to Christ on His Father's terms (i.e. in repentance and obedience). Only those who have been adopted as children of God are the recipients of the gift of salvation. Just an intellectual understanding about Jesus will not get you into Heaven. The way to identify and develop a personal relationship with Jesus is through doing the will of the Father, which is clearly explained within the teaching of Scripture, as outlined in the three EUCs. I now want to show you the importance and significance of the three EUCs from a proper Biblical perspective. They are as follows:

1. **Read** the Holy Bible daily. This is not a suggestion but is a command and the will of the Father. Reading God's Word is a necessity in the Christian faith — an essential element in our relationship with the Father — through Christ. The Holy Bible is the primary way that God communicates to His children (De. 6:5-6, 17:18-20; 1 Th. 5:27; 1 Ti. 4:13; 2 Ti. 2:15, 3:14-17, 4:2).

2. **Pray** to God daily. Prayer is commanded and the will of the Father (Ph. 4:6-7). Prayer is a form of serving God (Lk. 2:36-38) and obeying Him. Prayer is the primary method of communication between humans and a Triune God. This is why prayer is also an essential element in our relationship with the Father through Christ.

3. **Share** the Gospel of Jesus Christ regularly. This is a command and the will of the Father (Mt. 28:19-20). Christians are commanded to share their faith (Mk. 16:15) and to be ambassadors for Christ (2 Co. 5:17-21). The reason why we need to be obedient in sharing our faith is that obedience is evidence of salvation (He. 5:9). This

is why sharing our faith is an essential element in our relationship with the Father through Christ. To remain silent about the Gospel is a sin (Ja. 4:17).

Two Possibilities

Because of our relationship with The Triune God, the elements of the EUCs are vital and astronomically important within that relationship. I remind you again that these EUCs are **1.)** Reading the Bible daily, **2.)** Praying to God daily, and **3.)** Sharing our Faith regularly. These are all the will of the Father that we are commanded to obey — as followers of Jesus Christ. If you make the choice not to obey the will of God the Father, this action could very well be an indication that you are either a falsely converted individual, or else an elect in transition who has not been truly regenerated yet, and because of being either one of these, you would not have the capacity or the ability — or at least not yet have the capacity or ability — to understand the things of the Spirit of God (1 Co. 2:14).

Who Are the Elect?

Who are the elect before regeneration? The Apostle Paul tells us in Ephesians 2:1-5 where we read the following:

"¹And you were dead in your trespasses and sins, ²in which you used to walk when you conformed to the ways of this world and of the ruler of the power of the air, the spirit who is now at work in the sons of disobedience. ³All of us also lived among them at one time, fulfilling the cravings of our flesh and indulging its desires and thoughts. Like the rest, we were by nature children of wrath. ⁴But because of His great love for

us, God, who is rich in mercy, ⁵made us alive with Christ even when we were dead in our trespasses. It is by grace you have been saved!"

Also, in Ephesians 1:4-5 we read this:

"⁴For He chose us in Him before the foundation of the world to be holy and blameless in His presence. In love ⁵He predestined us for adoption as His sons through Jesus Christ, according to the good pleasure of His will."

The Call by God

Prior to their regeneration, even the elect are by nature children of wrath (Ep. 2:3-5), just like everyone else. The elect are under the same condemnation as everyone else before their *"Call by God"* to repentance has been implemented.[6] Until the elect are justified, they are under condemnation. When the elect receive their *"Call by God"*, at different times throughout world history they have the finished work of Christ on the cross (i.e. death and Resurrection) applied unto them. The elect sinner is under the temporary wrath of God, but he will never come under the eternal wrath of God. Even as a believer, the elect child of God can and will sin. When the child of God sins, he or she will be severely chastised by their loving Heavenly Father and brought back to the place of the narrow gate (Mt. 7:13-14). Until the elect are justified, they are unable to understand the things of God (1 Co. 2:14), but after justification they are decreed by God to be saved. Even before the elect have personally identified themselves as even being elect, it is possible that they could be actively involved within a religious community or institution unaware of their election. We see

---

6   The Westminster Confession of Faith 11:4; 13:1.

an example of this in Scripture. Paul himself lived a blameless life as a Pharisee (Ph. 3:5-6) until he received his call and regeneration by God on the road to Damascus. Also, after Paul's conversion, the Book of Acts tells us about multiple apologetic encounters at synagogues where the Holy Spirit, through Paul, persuaded many to believe the truth about Christ (Ac. 14:1, 17:2-3, 18), and they were regenerated. These people that The Holy Spirit persuaded through Paul were active already in the religious communities and institutions when the *"Call of God"* of regeneration was sent out and received by them.

The Majority

My point is this: that self-professing Christians are also busy in the Church today operating without the desires caused by the Holy Spirit that precede their good works, deeds, and actions, such as the three EUCs. According to most surveys that I have read recently, the majority of self-professing Christians in America do not read their Bible daily outside of church service(s); they seldom pray to God daily outside of church service(s); and they seldom, if ever, share the Gospel of Jesus Christ with a lost and dying world outside of church service(s).

Validated Premise

These above statistics completely validate the premise of this book, *Desires: Characteristics of True Conversion,* as outlined within the Essential Universal Characteristics (EUCs) which are the three essential spiritual *desires* that precede the physical manifestation of the good works of the Christian faith. These *desires* have been supernaturally implanted deep within the regenerated follower of Christ's conscience (i.e. heart, mind, soul, and spirit) by God the Holy Spirit at the moment of his or her regeneration and justification. The main premise of *Desires: Characteristics of True Conversion* is that the personal spiritual *desires* that precede the physical manifestation of our good works, deeds, and actions are the byproducts and indicators of true saving faith (Ja. 2:14), and that the absence of these *desires* is the lack of evidence of true saving faith!

The Discovery

In *Desires: Characteristics of True Conversion,* your understanding is important to me — that good works, deeds, and actions do not justify us or make us righteous before God, nor are they the means to salvation. In other words, true conversion is not caused by good works, but good works are caused by true conversion (i.e. regeneration). Due to the discovery of the EUCs, you can now personally recognize and identify the authenticity of your conversion at a personal level simply by observing the deep spiritual desires found internally within your conscience that precede the outward physical manifestation of your good works. That is really what this book is about in a nutshell — learning to authenticate true conversion (i.e. regeneration and justification) through the Holy Spirit's deeply implanted spiritual desires within the newly regenerated child of God's conscience that are identified and confirmed through the physical manifestation of our God-glorifying good works, deeds, and actions as outlined within the EUCs.

God's Desires and Will

It is God's desire and will that all disciples rightly divide the Word of Truth (2 Ti. 2:15), worship God in Spirit and in Truth

(Jn. 4:24), be ready to give an answer to anyone who asks about the hope that is in them with gentleness and respect (1 Pe. 3:15), and love God with all their heart, mind, soul, and strength (Mk. 12:30).

Understanding and Compliance

Without regeneration, and without the knowledge, understanding, and compliance to the EUCs, most of the will of the Father could not be understood or accomplished. The Word of God demonstrates and identifies to us how important the EUCs are in the life of authentic believers who have received the Supernatural embedment of the Holy Spirit-caused *desires* within us to compel and empower us to obey and to please God — doing His will. Some of these desires are as follows:

- Rightly dividing the Word of Truth (2 Ti. 2:15).
- Worshiping God in Spirit and in Truth (Jn. 4:24).
- Being ready to give an answer for the hope that is inside of us (1 Pe. 3:15).
- Loving God with all our heart, mind, soul, and strength (Mk. 12:30).
- Loving our neighbors as Christ loves us (Jn. 13:34).
- Giving thanks in everything (1 Th. 5:18).
- Believing and abiding in Jesus (Jn. 3:16-18).
- Abstaining from sexual immorality (1 Th. 4:3).
- Delighting in doing God's will (Ps. 40:3).
- Submitting in doing good (1 Pe. 2:13-15).
- Submitting to doing what we know is the right thing to do (Ja. 4:17).

Identification and Implementation

Distinguishing the difference between true and false conversions within our personal life will completely and absolutely be contingent upon the identification and implementation of the *desires* that were implanted deep within our conscience by God the Holy Spirit at the moment of our regeneration and justification which precede the physical manifestation of our good works, which include the implementation of the three EUCs identified in the Word of God. In other words, the good works of a genuine faith will always be preceded by the Holy Spirit-caused and Holy Spirit-powered *desires* — first and foremost — and then secondly by the corresponding physical manifestation of the good works that are based on the initial Holy Spirit-caused and Holy Spirit-driven desires that you received at the moment of your regeneration and justification.

Without Demonstration

When our Christian faith does not demonstrate or produce any outward physical manifestation of good works, deeds, and actions as taught in Scriptures and outlined in the EUCs — when good works, deeds, and actions are completely absent from a self-professing Christian's life — then the faith of this kind would be considered as a faith that is absent of the Holy Spirit. Because a faith that is absent of the Holy Spirit would logically be contrary to the will of the Father, this kind of faith would be identified not only as an incomplete faith, or an ineffective faith, but also the Apostle James actually considers this kind of faith to be a dead faith (Ja. 2:14-26). Question: Why does the Apostle James tell us that true faith will automatically produce good works, deeds, and actions? The reason why he does is that saving faith and works are interconnected in the Christian faith; they cannot be separated; and they still continue to be a Christian principle. The interconnection of faith and works is absolutely a reflection of an authentic, sincere, living, and saving faith — not a dead faith.

Three Questions

I want you to ask yourself these three questions of the EUCs. I want you to answer honestly for yourself, and doing so will give you a proper and correct understanding to the authenticity of your conversion. The three questions are as follows:

1. Do I have a *desire* to read the Holy Bible daily?

   Yes ☐ **No** ☐ **Seldom** ☐

2. Do I have a *desire* to pray to God daily?

   Yes ☐ **No** ☐ **Seldom** ☐

3. Do I have a *desire* to share the Gospel of Jesus Christ regularly?

   Yes ☐ **No** ☐ **Seldom** ☐

- If you honestly answered yes to all three of the EUCs questions above, then my book, *Desires: Characteristics of True Conversions,* is not intended for you, and Jesus would tell you, "Well done, good and faithful servant" (Mt. 25:23), and I would encourage you to please give this book to somebody else — perhaps a family member, friend, co-worker, or someone else you think will benefit from the content of this book.

- If you honestly answered yes to just one of the EUCs questions above, then this book is not specifically intended for you either, but could help you through the process of your sanctification, and I encourage you to continue to study the content of this book and to re-take the EUCs test again at a later date, after you have thoroughly studied the content of this book — alongside your Bible — so that you can improve your EUC score! Your score should absolutely be 100% — answering yes to all three questions!

- If you honestly answered no or seldom to all of the EUCs questions above, then this book is specifically intended for you, and you should be absolutely concerned about the authenticity of your regeneration and justification (i.e. true conversion). I encourage you to seek counsel from and pray with a pastor and/or elder and/or member of a healthy and well-balanced congregation in your community as soon as possible for now is the day of salvation (Is. 49:8; Ro. 1:16; 2 Co. 6:2).

Reasonable Conclusion

If we truly love God, we want to draw close to Him through reading His Word. If we truly love God, we want to draw close to Him through daily prayer. If we truly love God, we want to share Him with everyone around us. Because this is what God wants — this should be our greatest joy!

The Final Thought

I hope and pray that this book, *Desires: Characteristics of True Conversion,* has helped you to better understand the Biblical relationship between works and faith, and how to identify the difference between true and false conversion through the identification of both the spiritual and physical manifestations of the Essential Universal Characteristics (EUCs) of authentic regeneration. I hope that you understand that we are not saved by good works, deeds, and actions — but that good works, deeds, and actions are byproducts and indicators of true conversion (i.e. saving faith).

One thing that I want you to understand is that I believe that when our current physical life on earth is completed, and we are in the presence of the Lord Jesus Christ in Heaven, that Heaven will be filled with forgiven and regenerated sinners, and hell will not have any innocent people within it. I hope and pray this book has helped you to identify personally if, in fact, you are an authentically converted individual — positively identified as an adopted child of The Triune God!

Thank you for reading this book. Please contact Last Chance Music Ministry if you need a Bible at lastchancemusic1@aol.com, and my wife, Laura, and I will send you one — at no cost to you. The price has been paid in full!

In Christ,
David Meeker

Terms and Definitions

Adoption The giving to anyone the same name and privileges of a child who is not a child by birth. This term is found in the New Testament in Paul's letters. It is the process by which a man or woman might be brought into God's family, with all the same benefits and privileges through Jesus Christ (Jn. 1:12; Ro. 8:15, 23; Ep. 1:5; Ga. 3:26, 4:5;).

Apologetics The English word comes from a Greek root meaning "to defend, to make reply, to give an answer, to legally defend oneself." In the New Testament times apologia was a formal courtroom defense of something (2 Ti. 4:16).

Apostle A title referencing any of Jesus' 12 disciples after the resurrection of Christ, but sometimes referencing other Christ-followers with whom Jesus revealed Himself physically after the resurrection, such as Paul (Ac. 9:1-19, 22:6-21, 26:12-18).

Atonement The repair of the broken relationship between God and man restored by the death and resurrection of Jesus Christ (Ex. 12:5; Le. 17:11; Is. 53:3-12; Lu. 4:18, 19; Jn. 3:16; 10:17;

Ac. 20:28; Ro. 3:23-25; 1 Co. 7:23, 15:3; Ep. 2:13; Col. 1:12, 13; Tit. 2:14; He. 9:22; 1 Pe. 2:21-24, 3:18).

Belief The thing believed. Our belief is only as true, reliable, and good as the object in which it is placed. Christ is the object in which Christian belief is placed. Our Christian belief is in the person of Jesus Christ (Mk. 1:15; Ac. 20:21; Ro. 10:9; 2 Th. 2:13).

Body of Christ Christians make up the Body of Christ (1 Co. 12:27). Jesus is the head of the body (Col. 1:18) and should be the center of everything we say, do, and think (Mt.18:20). The Body of Christ meets together to pray (Ep. 6:18), worship (Ex. 34:14), share in suffering (2 Ti. 2:3), encourage (Ep. 4:12), and teach (2 Ti. 2:2) about Christ in love (Jn. 13:34) and unity (Ep. 4:3). The Body of Christ is responsible for the preaching of the Gospel to others (Mt. 28:18, 19) with gentleness and respect (1 Pe. 3:15).

Conversion The moment an individual repents and places his or her faith upon Jesus for his or her salvation. When the individual is declared righteous and forgiven by God, thus converted from being far from God to now being accepted and justified in Christ (2 Chr.7:14; Jn.3:5; Ac.2:38; Ro.12:2; Ep. 4:22; 2 Co. 5:17; Re. 3:20).

Covenant A treaty, or promise, between two people or groups. Biblically, it is a promise made by God to His people for salvation (Je. 31:31-34; Mt. 26:28; Lu. 22:20; He. 8:6, 8, 9:15, 12:24,13:20; 1 Co. 11:25).

Cult A cult is a religious group that denies one or more of the fundamentals of Biblical truth. Specifically, it is a group that claims to be Christian but whose teachings, if believed, would prevent someone from having a saving relationship with Jesus Christ (1Ti. 6:20; Col. 2:8).

Disciple A person who follows a teacher. This person does what his or her teacher says to do (Jn. 14:15; Lu. 11:28; 1 Jn. 5:3; 1 Ti. 6:14; Ja. 1:22).

Doctrine, Biblical A statement(s) describing a set of beliefs that is grounded in the Word of God and theologically sound.

Doubt A lack of faith or trust in something or someone. To not be sure (Pr. 3:5-8; Mt. 21:21; Ja. 1:5-8; Mk. 11:22-25; He. 11:6).

Doxology The study or act of worship by which believers ascribe worth, glory, and praise to God.

Election In the New Testament it occurs six times (Ro. 9:11, 11:5, 11:7, 28; 1 Th. 1:4; 2 Pe. 1:10). In all these passages it appears to denote an act of Divine selection upon human beings to bring them into a special and saving relationship with God.

Evil Bad. Wicked. Doing things that do not please God (Is. 5:20; Pr.8:13; Ro.3:23, 12:9; Ep. 6:12; 1 Th. 5:22).

Expiation Since the prefix *ex* means "out of" or "from," *expiation* has to do with removing something or taking something away. In Biblical terms, it has to do with taking away guilt through the payment of a penalty or offering of atonement.

Fact An isolated piece of information that is indisputable. Information used as evidence or as part of a news report, news article, or evidence in a legal court case.

Faith The on-going and personal commitment to trust and believe. What we believe. We can only be a Christian if we have faith in Christ (Ep. 3:7; Ga. 3:26). Our faith is the relationship we have with God through Jesus Christ (Jn. 14:6). Faith justifies not on its own worthiness and value, but by the worthiness and value of

Him in Whom is our faith (Ac. 20:21; Col. 2:9). Faith makes the connection, by which our sin is imputed to Christ, and Christ's righteousness is imputed to us (2 Co. 5:19, 21; 1 Co. 1:30). Without faith, we cannot please God (He. 11:6). We are saved by grace through faith in Christ (Ep. 2:8, 9).

Father, The God. The first person of the Trinity. The Father shares the same attributes and characteristics as Jesus and the Holy Spirit. He is holy (Is. 6:3; Le. 19:2), eternal (De. 33:27; Ps. 90:2), omnipresent (Ps. 139:7-12), omnipotent (Re. 19:6), omniscient (Ps. 139:2-6; Pr. 15:3), immutable (Mal. 3:6), righteous (Ps. 119:137), truth (Je. 10:10), good (Ps. 107:8), merciful (Ps. 103:8-17), gracious (Ps. 111:4), faithful (De. 7:9), and loves us (Jn. 3:16; 1 Jn. 4:8).

Forgiveness An act of pardon by God through the completed work of His Son Jesus Christ. It is a gift from God (Jn. 3:16; Ro. 6:23), through faith (Ep. 2:8, 9; Ro. 10:9, 10, 13) in Jesus Christ (Jn. 10:17). Forgiveness is promised by God when we repent of our sin and believe and trust in Jesus for our salvation (Jn. 3:16-18; 1 Jn. 1:8-10), but we have to forgive others if we want God to forgive us (Ep. 4:32).

God The Creator (Ge. 1:1) of the universe and everything that exists (Ac. 17:24). The Bible teaches that there is one God (1 Ti. 2:5) revealed in three persons — the Father, the Son, and the Holy Spirit (Mt. 3:16, 17; 1 Pe. 1:2) — Who all share the same attributes and characteristics. He is omnipresent (Ps. 139:7-12), omniscient (Ps. 139:2-6; Pr. 15:3), omnipotent (Re. 19:6), eternal (Ps. 45:6), holy (Is. 6:3), righteous (Ps. 119:137), merciful (Ps. 103:8-17), gracious (Ps. 111:4), faithful (De. 7:9), immutable

(Mal. 3:6), truthful (Je. 10:10), spirit (Jn. 4:24), good (Ps. 107:8), and love (1 Jn. 4:8).

Gospel, The Paul tells us what the Gospel is — that Christ died for our sin and was buried and rose again on the third day (1 Co. 15:3,4) to save us from the eternal consequences of our sin (Jn. 3:16). Salvation is a gift from God through faith in Jesus Christ (Ro. 6:23) because He loves us. The Gospel is the grace of God (Jn. 3:16-18; Ro. 1:16; Ac. 13:47, 16:17, 20:24; 1 Co. 15:2-6; Ep. 1:7; 1 Co. 1:30.)

Grace The loving act of God in a person's life, making possible his or her salvation, sanctification, and justification. It is by grace that God makes salvation possible through His Son Jesus Christ's death and resurrection (Ro. 6:23), and it is through grace that He sustains the Body of Christ (Ex. 34:6; Ep. 1:7, 8; 2:8, 9; 1 Pe. 1:13). Grace is a gift from God (Ro. 3:24). God's grace is revealed in His Gospel (Ac. 20:24).

Heaven The dwelling place of God and the hope and destiny of believers of Jesus Christ either by way of the grave or His coming (Is. 25:8; Mt. 5:17-20, 7:13, 14; Jn. 14:2, 3; 2 Co. 5:2; Ph. 1:23, 3:7; Col. 1:5; He. 8:1; 2 Pe. 3:13; Re. 7:17, 21:4, 22:5).

Hell A permanent place of torment for those who are condemned by sin because of their rejection of God's only provision for our sin, His Son Jesus Christ, where they are eternally separated from God in a place of torment (Mt. 8:12, 25:41; Ro. 1:18-20; 2 Pe. 2:4-9; Jude 1:7; Re. 21:8).

Hermeneutics The word *hermeneutics* comes from a Greek root meaning *"Interpreter"* or *"Interpret."* Thus, hermeneutics is an interpretation. *Merriam-Webster Dictionary* defines hermeneutics as *"the study of methodological principles of interpretation (as of the Bible)"* and *"a method or principle of interpretation."* It is also referred to as the *Art and Science of Biblical Interpretation.* The Holy Bible commands the followers of Christ in 2 Timothy 2:15 to be involved in hermeneutics. The five basic foundational rules of hermeneutics are as follows: **A.)** Scripture must be used to interpret itself. **B.)** Scripture itself is its best commentary. **C.)** Scripture must be taken literally allowing for normal use of figurative language, allegory, narrative, poetry, and parables. **D.)** Scripture must be interpreted in the context by which the passage was originally intended. Correct context will help with determining the correct meaning. **E.)** Be sensitive to the type of literature you are reading. Biblical hermeneutics must also follow these 15 fundamental rules:

1. Understand the author. (Who wrote the book?)
2. Understand the audience. (Why was the book written?)
3. Understand the meaning of words. (Strong's Dictionary or Bibleworks8 is recommended).
4. Understand the historical setting.
5. Understand the grammar.
6. Understand the textual issues.
7. Understand the syntax (the set of rules for the analysis or arrangement of words and phrases to create well-formed sentences in a language).
8. Understand the form and genre of the literature. (Is it legal, historical narrative, figures of speech, analogies, parables, Hebrew poetry and song, wisdom sayings and proverbs, the Gospels, prophecy, genealogy, letters or Epistles, Apocalyptic, etc.?)

9. Understand the immediate context (and remember a text out of context becomes a pretext).
10. Understand the document's context.
11. Understand the author's context.
12. Understand the Biblical context. (Biblical passages must be consistent with the whole of Scripture. Scripture is never contradictory of itself).
13. Understand the difference between prescriptive and descriptive statements in the Holy Bible. (Is the verse telling us to do something, or does it describe an action someone does?)
14. Build all doctrine on necessary rather than possible inferences. (A necessary inference is something that is clearly taught in Scripture. Its conclusion is conclusive. A possible inference is something that could or might be true — but not something actually stated by the text).
15. Interpret the unclear passages in Scripture in light of the clear.

God has given us His Holy Spirit to illuminate His Word and has created us with the ability to logically reason, which includes investigating, analyzing, and reviewing. To understand God's Word correctly is obviously one of the main reasons why God has equipped humans with the capacity for clear and sound reasoning in conducting or assessing factually based information according to strict principles of validity. Biblical interpretation implements the same rules found in the logical reasoning process. He has also given us many people throughout history to help us interpret His Word — which include gifted and anointed Bible teachers (Ep. 4:8-12).

Hypothesis A proposition not yet tested to the point of general acceptance. An un-scientifically supported theory.

Holy Spirit, The God. The third person of the Trinity active in creation (Ge. 1:2; Job 33:4; Ps. 104:30) and throughout history, indwelling believers (Ro. 8:11) and directing and guiding the Church (Jn. 16:12, 13) and is the Source of Scripture. The Holy Spirit shares the same attributes and characteristics in Scripture as the Father and Jesus Christ. He is omnipresent (Ps. 139:7-10), omniscient (Jn. 14:26, 16:12, 13), omnipotent (Lu. 1:35), eternal (He. 9:14), holy (Ro. 1:4), merciful (Ga. 5:22), immutable (Ga. 4:6), truthful (Jn. 16:13), and He teaches (Jn. 14:26), leads us (Ro. 8:14), gives us joy (1 Th. 1:6), seals us (Ep. 4:30), intercedes for us (Ro. 8:26), regenerates us (He. 9:14), reminds us (Jn. 14:26), reveals to us (1 Co. 2:10), communes with us (2 Co. 13:14; 1 Jn. 3:24), convicts us (Jn. 16:8-11) loves us (Ro. 5:5; 15:30; Ga. 5:22), is involved in salvation (Tit. 3:5), and sanctifies us (Ro. 15:16). The Holy Spirit's ministry is both personal and permanent (Jn. 14:16-17).

Imago Dei The Latin translation of "image of God," this term is used to describe God creating mankind in His image and likeness (Ge. 1:26-28), resulting in every single person having immense worth, value, and the unique ability to reflect and connect with God the Creator.

Image of God When the Bible uses the terminology, "created in the image of God" (Ge. 1:26-28), it is talking about the fact that people are made in God's image comprised of mind, emotion, and will. We are able to perceive and feel things and have conscience knowledge of our own abilities and character, having self-aware-ness. We are moral beings with an inborn 'moral compass," which was given to us from God, as a natural orientation of 'right' and 'wrong.' We have instinctive capacity to develop and appreciate beauty, drama, art, and story in all forms; and we will naturally seek out and develop relationships and friendships with others. We are all this because God is all this and we are made in God's image and likeness. All these conclusions are consistent with what we observe about ourselves in reality and the overall teachings of the Holy Bible.

Jesus Christ. God The second person of the Trinity. The Creator of the universe and everything that exists (Jn. 1:1-3; Col. 1:16, 17). He is sinless (2 Co. 5:21; 1 Jn. 3:5). Jesus shares the same attributes and characteristics in Scripture as the Father and Holy Spirit. He is omnipresent (Mt. 18:20; 28:18-20), omniscient (Jn. 16:30, 21:17), omnipotent (He. 1:3), eternal (Jn. 1:1, 2, 17:5, 24), holy (Lu. 1:35), righteous (1 Jn. 2:1), merciful (Jude 1:21), faithful (Re. 1:5), immutable (He. 13:8), truthful (Jn. 14:6), good (Lu. 18:18, 19), gracious (1 Pe. 2:3), and loves us (Jn. 15:13; Ga. 2:20). Jesus is called God in the New Testament (Jn. 1:1,; 10:20-33, 20:28; Ro. 9:5; Col. 2:9; Tit. 2:13; He. 1:8).

Judgment God will bring every work and secret thing into judgment, whether good or evil, believer or non-believer (Da. 7:10; Job 34:23; Ps. 9:7; Ec. 3:17, 11:9, 12:14; Mal. 3:5; Mt. 12:36, 25:32; Jn. 5:24, 7:24; Ro. 14:10; 1 Co. 3:12-15; 2 Co. 5:10; 2 Ti. 4:8; He. 9:27, 12:23; Re. 11:18, 20:11-15).

Justification The gift of God by which He restores us to a right relationship with Himself through the death and resurrection of His Son Jesus Christ (1 Jn. 1:9, 2:23, 24, 5:1; Ro. 3:23, 24).

Law, Scientific A statement describing how some phenomena of nature behave. Laws are generalizations from data. They express regularities and patterns in the data. A law is usually limited in scope, to describe a particular process in nature.

Mediator Jesus Christ stands between God and men in establishing our relationship with God. Jesus is the guarantee of our relationship with God. Jesus Christ is the only mediator between God and men (Jn. 14:6; Ac. 4:12; 1 Ti. 2:5).

Messiah A Hebrew word that means "The Anointed One." It means the same thing as the Greek word *Christ*. See also Jesus.

Mercy God's mercy and compassion to help those in need or in distress. God's mercy cannot be separated from His love, grace, and faithfulness. God's ultimate mercy was shown through His willingness to send His Son Jesus Christ as a sacrifice for the world (Mi. 6:8; Lu. 6:36; Ro. 11:30; Ep. 2:4; 1 Ti. 1:2; 2 Ti. 1:2; Tit. 3:5; 1 Pe. 1:3, 2:10; Jude 1:21; 1 Jn.1:3).

Obey To do what you are told to do. To carry out God's commands. According to Scripture, God demands that His revelation be taken as a rule for man's whole life in both heart and conduct (Je. 7:22; 1 Sa. 15:22; 1 Co. 14:21; Tit. 3:1). The disobedience of Adam and Eve plunged mankind into guilt, condemnation, and death (Ro. 5:19; 1 Co. 15:22). Christ's unfailing obedience "unto death" (Ph. 2:8; He. 5:8, 10:5-10) won righteousness (acceptance with God) and life (fellowship with God) for all who believe on Him (Ro. 5:15-19). Faith in the Gospel — and in Jesus Christ — is obedience (Ac. 6:7; Ro. 6:17; He. 5:9; 1 Pe. 1:22) — for God commands it (Jn. 6:29; 1 Jn. 3:23). A life of obedience to God is the fruit of faith (Ge. 22:18; He. 11:8, 17; Ja. 2:22). Unbelief is disobedience (Ro. 10:16; 2 Th. 1:8; 1 Pe. 2:8, 3:1, 4:17).

Paradise A perfect place. Another name used for Abraham's bosom or Heaven (Lu. 16:19-31, 23:43; 2 Co. 12:3; Re. 2:7).

Pardon The forgiveness of sins granted freely by God as a gift (Ro. 3:23) through faith in Jesus Christ (Is. 43:25; Ps. 65:3; Ps. 86:5; Is. 1:18; Eze. 36:25; Mt. 6:14, 15, 18:21-35; Col. 3:13; 1 Jn. 1:8, 9).

Prayer Prayer is talking with and being with God. Through adoration, confession, thanksgiving, and supplication, believers are able to worshipfully communicate with God in order to build intimacy with Him (Je. 29:12; Ph. 4:6; Ps. 102:17; Ja. 5:16; Mt. 6:6; 26:41; Lu. 6:27-28; 1 Th. 5:16-18; 1 Jn. 1:9).

Propitiation The removal of God's judgment on mankind through the death and resurrection of Jesus Christ (Jn. 3:16; 1 Jn. 5:3, 11).

Reconciliation Man is restored to God through Christ to friendship and harmony. When Christ died on the cross, He satisfied God's judgment and made it possible for God's enemies to reconcile with Him (Ro. 5:10; 2 Co. 5:18-20; Col. 1:20, 21).

Redemption The restoring of our fellowship with God through Jesus Christ's death and resurrection (Jn. 3:16-18; Col. 1:13, 14; He. 9:12).

Regeneration Believers are new creations through their belief in the Gospel of Jesus Christ as they commit and dedicate their lives to Jesus Christ (Jn. 15:4-9; 2 Co. 5:17).

Religion A fundamental set of beliefs and practices generally agreed upon by a like-minded group of people. This set of beliefs concerns the cause, nature, and purpose of the universe, and involves devotional and ritual observances. It also often contains a moral code governing the conduct of human affairs, also known as a worldview (1 Co.2:1-5; Col. 2:8).

Repentance Confession of and turning away from our sin through the conviction of the Holy Spirit and turning to God for mercy through Jesus Christ with a desire to obey and serve Him (Eze.18:30; Mt. 3:2; 4:17; Lu. 3:7, 8, 13:3-5; Jn. 16:8; Ac. 2:38, 3:19, 8:22, 17:30; 2 Co. 7:9, 10; 2 Pe. 3:9).

Salvation Salvation refers to the process of sinners becoming justified, sanctified, and glorified through the death and resurrection of Jesus Christ — deliverance from the physical and spiritual bondage of sin by God's grace through faith in Jesus Christ and His completed work on the cross. Salvation is a gift from God, by grace, through faith, and cannot be achieved through self-effort – but only through Christ (Jn. 1:12, 13, 3:1-18, 14:6, 17:1-5; Ac. 2:37, 38; Ro. 6:23, 10:8-10; 2 Co. 7:10; Ep. 2:1-9; Col. 1:13, 14; 1 Th. 5:9; Tit. 2:11; He. 5:9; 1 Pe. 1:18, 19).

Sanctification The completing to perfection the work begun in regeneration, and it extends to the whole person (Ro. 6:9, 13, 22; 1 Co. 1:30, 6:19, 20; 2 Co. 4:6; Col. 3:10; 1 Th. 4:3; 2 Th. 2:13; 1 Pe. 1:2; 1 Jn. 4:7).

Sin To disobey or displease God. Lawlessness (1 Jn. 3:4), the result of disobedience (Ro. 5:19) and rebellion (Is. 1:2) against God. Sin is unbelief (1 Jn.1:10). The result of sin is death (Ro. 5:12). Jesus Christ is God's remedy for sin (2 Co. 5:21). Christ has saved us from the power, control, and consequences of sin, and from eternal separation from God (Ge. 3:1-19; Ps. 51; Ro. 3:23; 6:23; 1 Jn. 1:8, 9).

Soul A person's true inner self.

Theory A supposition or system of ideas intended to explain something, especially one based on general principles independent of the thing to be explained. A model (usually mathematical) that links and unifies a broader range of phenomena, and that links and synthesizes the laws that describe those phenomena. In science they do not grant an idea the status of theory until its consequences have been very well tested.

The Trinity The word *Trinity* is not used in the Holy Bible, but the concept is throughout. For example: **1)**. Who raised Jesus from the dead? Well, it was God the Father (Ga. 1:1; 1 Th. 1:10); it was also Jesus Himself (Jn. 2:19, 10:17, 18; and it was the Holy Spirit (Ro. 8:11). **2)**. Who gave the New Covenant? The Father (Je. 31:33, 34), Jesus (He. 8:1-13, 10:29, 12:24, 13:20), and the Holy Spirit (He. 10:15-17) gave the New Covenant. **3)**. Who sanctifies believers? The Father (1 Th. 5:23), Jesus (He. 13:12), and the Holy Spirit (1 Pe. 1:2) sanctify believers. **4)**. Who is the Creator? The Father (Ge. 1:1; Is. 44:24; Ac. 17:24; Ep. 3:9), Jesus (Jn. 1:3; Col. 1:16; He. 1:2), and the Holy Spirit (Job 33:4) are the Creator. **5)**. Who indwells believers? The Father (1 Co. 3:16a; 2 Co. 6:16; 1 Jn. 3:24), Jesus (Jn. 6:56; Ro. 8:10; Ep. 3:17), and the Holy Spirit (Jn.14:16, 17; Ro. 8:9, 11; 1 Co. 3:16b) indwell believers. The Holy Bible even describes this in terms of different combinations — Father and Son (Jn. 14:23), Father and Holy Spirit (Ep. 2:21, 22; 1 Jn. 3:24), and Son and Holy Spirit (Ga. 4:6).

Witnessing In the New Testament, believers are instructed to be a good witness with both our speech and our lifestyle (1 Ti. 4:12; Ga. 5:22, 23) — sharing our faith with others (Is. 52:7; Eze. 3:18, 19; Mt. 5:14-16, 28:18-20; Lu. 12:8, 9; Ac. 1:8; 1 Co. 3:5-9; 2 Co. 5:18-21; 1 Pe. 3:15).

Worldview A perspective of reality itself, a view of life, a comprehensive conception or apprehension of the world from a specific point of view. A worldview is a formal philosophy. The Christian worldview is consistent and non-contradictory and explains all the facts of our life's experiences. Every individual has a worldview, a perspective that both interprets and influences one's life. A worldview consciously or subconsciously answers four questions; **1.)** Who am I? (What is the nature of human beings?), **2.)** Where am I? (What is the nature of the world?), **3.)** What is wrong? (What is the nature of evil?), and **4.)** What is the solution? (What is the nature of good and salvation?)

Personal Notes

Personal Notes

Personal Notes

Personal Notes

_____

_____

_____

_____

_____

_____

_____

_____

_____

_____

_____

_____

_____

Please contact us at lastchancemusic1@aol.com if you need a Bible and we will send you one at no cost. The price has been paid in full.

Deepen your relationship with God through a better understanding of His Word using LCMM materials (books and music) that glorify God, edify the Body of Christ, and reach a lost and dying world.

BOOKS

In Christ's Service: A Concise Biblical Approach. This book will help you to better understand what it means to be a disciple of Christ in His service, answering many important questions, such as **1.)** What does it mean to be a disciple? **2.)** How can I please God with my life? **3.)** How can I get closer to God? **4.)** Is obedience important to God? **5.)** Should I share my faith with others? And many more!

Get your copy today at Amazon.com. Available in eBook only for $4.99.

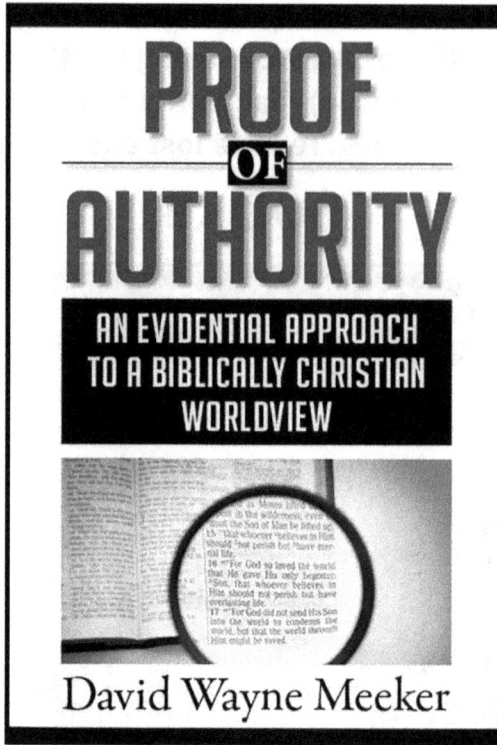

Proof of Authority: An Evidential Approach to a Biblically Christian Worldview Biblical Christianity is the only religion in the world that provides with its message *Proof of Authority*. God gives us overwhelming internal and external evidence in the coherency, accuracy, and unity of His word as it relates to our reality in validating His message. When you see all the evidence presented in this book, you will find a strong and irrefutable case for the Divine Origin and Inspiration of the Holy Bible.

Get your copy today at Amazon.com. Available in paperback $16.99, hardcover $21.99, and eBook $4.99.

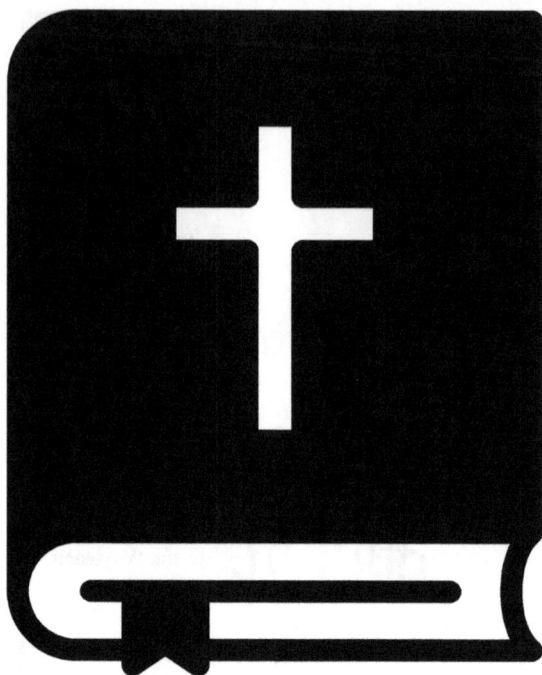

The Holy Bible is the most important Book that you can ever read. Please contact Last Chance Music Ministry at lastchance-music1@aol.com and we will send you a copy of *The Holy Bible* at no cost to you. The price has been paid in full!

CHRISTIAN MUSIC

Played on Christian radio (KNLE 88.1 FM) in Austin, Texas.

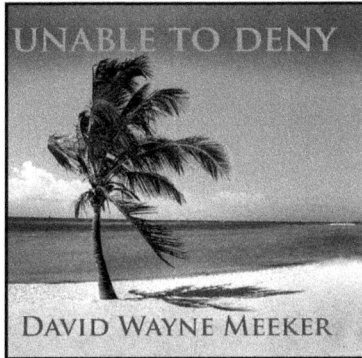

Unable to Deny CD; music available for digital downloads only.

Category: Christian Music. 10 songs total — all originals. Available at digital music download sites, including Apple Music, Amazon.com, Pandora, Shazam, Spotify, YouTube, Boomplay Music, Google Play, and many more!

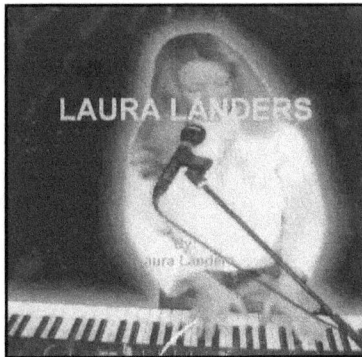

Laura Landers CD; music available at Amazon.com and Apple Music.

Category: Christian Music. 12 songs total — all originals. Laura had this album recorded before we got married and it is one of my favorites!

www.ingramcontent.com/pod-product-compliance
Lightning Source LLC
Chambersburg PA
CBHW071132090426
42736CB00012B/2101